How to produce synthwa

By Kaikani Laigo, a.k.a. Aquamaster

Universityofmetastudies.com

Foreword

I. Introduction
- 1.1 Explanation of the genre of synthwave
- 1.2 What kind of computer do I need?
- 1.3 Overview what's needed to produce synthwave music at home
- 1.4 Overview of the writing and recording process

II. Setting Up Your Home Studio

- 2.1 Choosing and setting up a digital audio workstation (DAW)
- 2.2 Studio monitors
- 2.3 Using and installing Reaper
- 2.4 Reaper basics
- 2.5 Free Plug-ins
- 2.6 Paid Plug-ins
- 2.7 Hardware vs. Software Synthesizers
- 2.8 MIDI controllers
- 2.9 Supplemental info: What is a ROMpler?
- 2.10 What synthesizer do I get?
- 2.11 Free VST Synths and drums
- 2.12 Outboard preamps
- 2.13 Tips for creating a comfortable and efficient workspace

III. Music Theory and Composition
- 3.1 A word on composing music
- 3.2 The Piano Roll
- 3.3 Intervals and chords
- 3.4 Basic music theory and chord progressions
- 3.5 Song key and moods
- 3.6 Composing a Drum Beat
- 3.7 Composing a Bass Line
- 3.8 How to create and sequence melodies and harmonies
- 3.9 Arranging and structuring a song
- 3.10 How to Build a 3rd harmony

IV. Sound Design
- 4.1 Techniques for creating and shaping synth sounds
- 4.2 Examples of synthwave sounds
- 4.3 Using samples and drum machines
- 4.4 Bass synth sound design
- 4.5 Adding effects such as reverb and delay
- 4.6 Analog Synth Controls

Foreword

I struggled with the idea of writing this book for a while. Traditionally, books on audio engineering or "music production" aren't genre-specific, and for mostly good reasons– The core principles of recording music are somewhat universal. Objectively, it doesn't matter if you're recording rock, pop, or rap… the goal is to record your source instruments and vocals as accurately as possible. However, I feel that the role of the modern-day bedroom producer (regardless of success level) is much more subjective, and that modern workflows require artistic decisions to be made simultaneously with production and engineering decisions. The roles of "artist" and "producer" are necessarily taken on by the same person, so there is (in my opinion) now a great benefit to studying the nuts-and-bolts art of audio engineering alongside the more creative aspects that lend themselves to a specific musical genre.

In this case, that genre would be synthwave and/or retrowave. I will use those terms somewhat interchangeably in this book, but will also try to delineate between the two genres where appropriate. If not yet familiar, synthwave tends to describe the more "modern" or futuristic sounding music, while "retrowave" is describing music that sticks to a more strict emulation of the 1980s aesthetic. While I am no means an expert on synthwave music, I have released several albums worth of synthwave and retrowave music (among other genres), and was also around during the 1980s in person. My synthwave music under the name "Aquamaster" has had a decent amount of critical acclaim and traction amongst fans of the genre, so that I feel counts for something. More importantly, I have been producing original music and composing electronic rock, pop, and heavy metal music consistently for over three decades, and I have also worked in the music instrument retail space. All of that experience gives me a fairly decent understanding of what you will need to set up a home studio and compose synthwave music (or most any type of electronic music) in the comfort of your own living space.

Part I: Introduction

1.1 Explanation of Synthwave:

Synthwave, also known as "outrun" or "retrowave", is a genre of electronic music that emerged in the early 2000s. The style is heavily influenced by the music and aesthetics of the 1980s, specifically the synth-heavy pop and film soundtrack music of that era. However, synthwave quickly grew beyond being simply a musical revival, and is now a genre in its own right. In fact, most of what is considered to be modern synthwave is objectively rather far removed from music that was produced in the 1980s. To a degree, the synthwave community also exists independently of traditional "electronic dance music". In my opinion, this is because many synthwave artists come from musical backgrounds outside of traditional EDM, such as metal, classic rock, and pop.

One of the defining characteristics of synthwave is its use of vintage synthesizers, such as the Roland Jupiter-8 and the Yamaha DX7. These instruments are used to create the genre's distinctive retro sound, which often includes lush, atmospheric pads and soaring, melodic lead synth lines. Retro drum machines and drum-machine samples are also used, often borrowing from the classic sounds of Alesis, Boss, Roland, and Linn drum machines.

Another key aspect of synthwave is its visual aesthetic, which is heavily influenced by the aesthetics of the 1980s, particularly the neon-lit, futuristic look of films like Blade Runner and Tron. Probably the most commonly used motif in synthwave imagery is that of the sun with horizon lines, often done in a color gradient, and often with some sort of "grid landscape" in the foreground. This has been sometimes referred to as the "synthwave sun" or "grid world", and in my opinion is a bit overused at this point. I'll admit, I unashamedly used my own version of this visual motif on the cover of one of my own albums, as well as the cover of this very book. This aesthetic is often reflected in the music videos, album artwork, and live performances of other synthwave artists as well. I guess if it's not broken, don't fix it... right?

Musically, synthwave is influenced by the new and electronic-laden music of the 80s, artists such as (in no particular order) Jan Hammer, Vangellis, Jean-Michael Jarre, Wendy Carlos, Duran Duran, Human League, Giorgio Moroder, Gary Numan, as well as soundtrack artists such as John Carpenter and Paul Hertzog. There is also an undeniable rock influence, especially among a certain sub-set of synthwave artists and producers. These influences would include 80s rockers such as Journey, Stan Bush, Def Lepard, Robert Tepper, and Survivor.

While synthwave has its roots in the 1980s, the genre has evolved to include a variety of sub-genres and influences. Some synthwave artists incorporate elements of other electronic music genres such as electro, techno, and even trip-hop into their sound. Additionally, many synthwave artists draw inspiration from other decades, such as the 1990s, and incorporate elements of genres like house and trance music.

The origins of the synthwave can be traced back to the early 2000s, when a group of musicians began to experiment with creating electronic music inspired by the soundtracks of 1980s films and video games. One of the first and most notable synthwave artists is Kavinsky, whose 2006 EP "1986" is considered to be one of the first synthwave releases.

The genre gained popularity in the 2010s, with the release of several influential albums and the emergence of a thriving online community of synthwave enthusiasts. Notable synthwave artists include PYLOT, Com Truise, Mitch Murder, The Midnight, Lazerhawk, and others.

In recent years, synthwave has also found its way into mainstream media, with its sound and aesthetic being featured in films, television shows, and video games. The genre has also had an impact on other styles of music, with many pop, hip-hop, and rock artists incorporating synthwave elements into their sound.

Overall, synthwave is a genre of music that pays homage to the nostalgia of the 1980s, combining vintage synthesizers and drum machines with modern production techniques to create a unique, nostalgic sound that continues to evolve and inspire new artists.

1.2 What kind of computer do I need?

First and foremost, you need a suitable computer to get up and running. This along with your audio interface are the heart and brains of your studio set-up. When it comes to recording music on a computer, there are a few key components to consider in terms of hardware requirements. These include the processor, RAM, and hard drive.

The processor is the brain of the computer, responsible for running all the programs and software. For music production, a minimum of a quad-core processor is recommended. This will ensure that your computer can handle the demands of running a Digital Audio Workstation (DAW) software and various audio plug-ins.

RAM, or Random Access Memory, is another important component to consider. RAM is responsible for allowing the computer to quickly access and process data. For music production, a minimum of 8GB of RAM is recommended. This will ensure that your computer can handle the demands of running a DAW software and various audio plug-ins without slowing down or freezing.

Hard drive is a storage device in the computer where your music files, DAW software, and plug-ins are stored. A minimum of 256GB of storage is recommended for music production. This will ensure that you have enough space to store all your files, including large audio samples and plug-ins, without running out of space.

In addition to the above requirements, a computer meant for music production should also have a good quality audio interface, and a good quality monitor. A good quality audio interface will ensure that the audio quality is high and that the computer can handle multiple audio inputs and outputs. A good quality monitor will ensure that the audio is displayed correctly and that you can see the audio levels and waveforms.

In summary, the minimum requirements for a computer meant for music production are:

- A quad-core processor
- 8GB of RAM
- 256GB of hard drive space

These are really the bare-bones requirements, but meeting these requirements should enable you to run some DAW software and various audio plug-ins, and allow you to record, edit and produce music with a high quality. Personally, with the rise of more complex A.I. driven plug-ins, I would go with the following as a "minimum":

- A quad-core processor
- 16GB of RAM
- 500GB of hard drive space

Also remember that when it comes to a studio computer, more is more. More (and faster) processors mean you can run more plug-ins, and more complex plug-ins simultaneously. Modern software synthesizers can be absolute CPU hogs. More ram is also better for your entire operation to run smoothly, and more hard drive storage means you have more space to record songs. A desktop is also going to be better than a laptop in almost every scenario, unless you really *have* to stay mobile on a daily basis.

1.3 Overview what's needed to produce synthwave music at home

I'm going to try and stick with the basics here. It's really easy to go overboard (most producers eventually do). In truth, you don't need much, though I am going to assume that you already have a capable PC or Mac desktop or laptop computer (not a tablet, or a smartphone). Producing synthwave music at home requires a combination of both hardware and software. Here is an overview of the equipment and software you will need to get started:

1. Digital Audio Workstation (DAW) - This is the software you will use to compose, record, edit, and mix your music. Some popular options include Reaper, Ableton Live, FL Studio, and Logic Pro. It is important to choose a DAW that you feel comfortable using and that has the features you need, since it is the single most important piece of gear on this list, and is utterly necessary for the purposes of this book. It is assumed that you also have a computer capable of running your chosen DAW and any accompanying plug-ins. Modern computers are usually up to the task

2. Synthesizer - A synthesizer is a crucial piece of equipment for producing synthwave music. Some popular options include the Roland JP-08, the Moog Minimoog, and the Korg MS-20. Software synthesizers such as Omnisphere, Serum, and DIVA can also be used in DAW.

3. Audio Interface - This is perhaps the single most important piece of gear that you need, second only to your computer/DAW. An audio interface is a small outboard hardware unit that is used to connect your synthesizer, drum machine, and other pieces of equipment to your computer. The interface will have one or more inputs that are suitable for microphones and/or instruments. It will also have separate outputs for your studio monitors and your headphones. The interface attaches to your computer via a USB cable, and is needed to get audio in and out of your computer's DAW in a professional manner. In many ways, the interface is the heart of your studio set-up.. Some popular options include the Focusrite Scarlett 2i2, the PreSonus AudioBox, and the Universal Audio Apollo.

4. MIDI Controller - A MIDI controller is a device that allows you to control the parameters of your synthesizer and drum machine using knobs, sliders, or keys. Most MIDI controllers are in the form-factor of a traditional keyboard, while others have percussion pads and alternative input surfaces. Some popular options include the Akai MPK Mini, the Novation Launchkey, the Novation Launchpad, and the Korg nanoKontrol.

5. Studio Monitors - Studio monitors are speakers that are designed for use in a recording studio. They provide a more accurate representation of the sound than regular speakers, which is essential for mixing and mastering your music. Most studio monitors are sold separately, and purchased in pairs. Many home studios use two-way speakers, meaning there are two separate speakers for the high and midrange frequencies. Most home studios use either 5" or 8" monitors, which is the size of the main driver (speaker). 8" speakers provide better bass response, but are often too loud for small rooms. While many beginners believe they can do all their work on headphones, this is a rookie mistake since headphones aren't accurate enough to make critical mixing decisions with. Some popular options include the KRK Rokit 5 G4, Yamaha HS5, Kali Audio IN-5, and the JBL Professional 305P MkII.

6. Microphone - A microphone is not essential if you're only recording synthwave instrumentals, but it can be useful for recording vocals or other live instruments. Some

popular options include large diaphragm condenser mics like the Audio-Technica AT2020 and Rode NT1-A, while others prefer the lower sensitivity of dynamic mics, like the Shure SM7B, and the Electro-Voice RE20

7. Headphones - Headphones are essential for monitoring your music and for making precise adjustments during the mixing and mastering process. They are also indispensable if you plan on working on your music at night, or in private, or if you are recording vocals. Studio headphones come in several styles, mainly "semi-open" and "closed", which refers to the style of the speaker housing that goes over the wearer's ear. I prefer closed headphones, because when I'm recording vocals they greatly reduce the amount of sound that bleeds into the microphone. Some popular options include the Sony MDR-7506, Beyerdynamic DT 990 Pro, the Sennheiser HD 660 S, and the AKG K712 Pro.

You also don't need to buy everything at once. You can conceivably start your journey with an audio interface, a DAW (one that includes virtual instruments), and headphones. Of course this would assume that you're going to step-record all of your MIDI, and you won't have monitors to make professional-quality final mixes. However, you can buy monitors later (when you're ready to mix), and you can also buy plug-ins and virtual instruments as needed.

Optional equipment:

Here are some optional items that you technically don't need to make synthwave, but you may really want, or find useful in creating your own sound. Keep in mind that most professional and semi-pro producers have a lot of stuff, as they acquire instruments and pieces of gear over the years. Whether it's virtual instruments and plug-ins, classic instruments like electric pianos, organs, and guitars, or rooms full of keyboard and rackmount hardware synths- these are all options that you can freely explore when you've stock piled them.

Similarly, many pro-musicians like to try new gear and technology, and many times it isn't for them... but you won't know if you don't try it out. While it may be more economical to "try before you buy", I guess I'm saying don't feel bad about trying new gear that doesn't work out for you personally. In most cases you can return new items under warranty, or sell used items on the 2nd hand market for a minimal loss. This actually isn't the case with software items (like plug-ins), although many of those have free trial periods that allow you to "try before you buy".

Here are some additional pieces of gear that you will probably find in many advanced synthwave studio set-ups.

8. A guitar - This is actually my first recommendation for a piece of gear that isn't actually necessary. This entry also includes bass guitars, acoustic guitars, and really any sort of supplemental stringed instrument, but my choice (for making synthwave) would be an electric guitar. This is because guitars are actually a pretty big part of retrowave music, and because the sound of a real electric guitar is one of those things that's still fairly

hard to emulate well. Lastly, cheap electric guitars are being manufactured at a higher quality than they ever were in the past. Most "entry level" guitars from decent brands are more than sufficient to record with these days. My advice as a guitarist of over 30 years- If you prefer classic 80s pop guitar sounds, particularly clean tones, get a stratocaster or strat-style guitar with three single coil pickups. If you are into heavier tones, and want a true "heavy metal" guitar sound, then choose a guitar with two humbucker pickups.

9. Expensive plug-ins - While you will certainly have to buy some plug-ins, there are a lot that you will not have to purchase as they will likely come bundled with your DAW. However, there is a lot to be said for the phrase "you get what you pay for". High-end plug-ins are expensive, and they tend to sound better. In fact (and I'm being honest here), there are going to be very few instances where the difference between a "free" plug-in, and the professionally expensive one will not be hugely significant. And by significant, I mean "oh my goodness, how did I ever do this before???", or "wow, that sounds WAY better!". There are of course times when a free version of a plug in is exceptional, and 100% usable. A lot of times free plug-ins are hit-or-miss, though. In this book, I will give examples and recommendations for free plug-ins when applicable. With that said, it's not a bad idea to invest some money in plug-ins (even where not completely necessary).

10. Hardware drum machine and/or extra drum software - A drum machine is another not-quite essential (but highly sought after) piece of equipment for producing synthwave music. Some popular options include the Roland TR-808 and the LinnDrum. Like hardware synths, a lot of people prefer the tactile nature of hardware drum machines. Also, some hardware units employ analog circuits and filters that certain producers swear by. Oftentimes hardware drum machines are small, portable, have great sounds, and are relatively cheap on the used market... which can make them a very tempting and worth-whille investment. Specialty software drum machines such as EZDrummer and Addictive Drums can also be purchased and used in a DAW. Both of those programs focus on emulating a live drummer, so they might not be particularly suited for a synthwave project. Also keep in mind that we will need at least one software drum machine once we begin, so on some level a drum machine is actually necessary.

11. An MPE MIDI controller - While these might not be extremely commonplace now, they're a lot of fun and I suspect that they will be a fairly normal studio fixture in the times to come. MPE (MIDI Polyphonic Expression) controllers are MIDI controllers that are designed to offer a more expressive and dynamic playing experience. MPE controllers typically have multiple dimensions of touch-sensitivity, such as pressure, slide, and bend, which can be assigned to different parameters of a sound. This allows for more expressive performance and control over the sounds being produced. MPE controllers can be used with MPE-enabled software or hardware synthesizers to provide more realistic and expressive performances. Examples of MPE controllers include LinnStrument, Roli Seaboard, and Roger Linn Design's Linnstrument.

In addition to the equipment listed above, you may also want to consider purchasing things like specialty MIDI controllers, extra computer monitors, more guitars, guitar effects, amps, extra microphones, studio furniture, etc. The list really never ends. In producer circles, there's a thing called "G.A.S.", which stands for "Gear Acquisition Syndrome". While most of this stuff is useful and lots of fun, it's important to not get too caught up in buying gear, and keep your eyes on the prize (making music!). There's nothing that gets made fun of more in musician circles than the guy who "has everything" but somehow is never able to put together a finished track. Don't be that guy. Focus on what is necessary for now, and remember that with the right equipment and software, you can start producing synthwave music at home and create professional-sounding tracks.

1.4 Overview of the writing and recording process

Here's a quick breakdown of what we have planned. Think of this as a roadmap to better guide you through the rest of this book. Don't be intimidated if this does not immediately make sense to you– as we go through the following chapters, this "map" will begin to make more sense, and the steps will be explained in detail.

I should also explain that there are many other workflows and as you grow as a recording artist you will eventually discover what works for you. Some musicians write a song out in its entirety before ever stepping foot in a recording studio. Others will demo-record a song several times, often completely changing instruments, and recording methods before actually buckling down and recording a final version. In fact, these approaches used to be standard in the days before high-quality home studios. For the purpose of this book, we will be writing our song's parts as we record them. I figure it is best to write and record our demo song essentially at the same time, since this is the quickest and most practical way to the finish line, and also because our composition requirements are fairly simple.

Get in the car (probably a DeLorean)... we're making synthwave in 12 easy steps:

1. Get your studio set up, and connect your audio interface to your computer.

2. Play around with your sounds and synths. Save some presets.

3. Start recording as soon as you have some musical concepts in mind! I'll give you some ideas, and quantization will be your friend.

4. Track a drum part

5. Overdub a bass synth part using our multitrack DAW.

6. Add chords over your bass line using it as a guide.

7. Create some other parts and instrumentation.

8. Time to arrange your song!

9. Make sure everything is in time and in tune.

10. Add more embellishments if necessary

11. Mix and master your track!

12. Self-publish and promote your music.

It might sound simple, and it sort of is if you can stick with me long enough. Let's start with building your home studio set-up.

Part II: Setting up your Home Studio

2.1 Choosing and setting up a DAW

Choosing and setting up a digital audio workstation (DAW) is an essential step when setting up a home studio for producing synthwave music. A DAW is the software that you will use to compose, record, edit, and mix your music. It's important to know that generally speaking, there isn't a huge difference between most major DAWs. While it's true that out of the thousands of common features they all share, there are a few features here and there that are unique, but for the most part they all do exactly the same thing. Digital audio is digital audio, so DAWs don't typically "color the sound" or sound different from one to the next. They all record and playback audio and MIDI in essentially the same way.

The main differences between them essentially come down to the GUI layout, workflow specifics, and bundled plug-ins. In fact, that is probably the single most important factor when deciding what DAW to buy- what plug-ins it comes with. Some DAWs come stock with literally everything you need, such as Ableton or FL studio. Other choices, like Reaper, come with much fewer stock plug-ins, and the expectation there is that you will use it with 3rd party plug-ins of your choice. Personally I prefer this, as I can choose better-than-stock virtual synths that suit me better. There are many different DAW options available, each with its own unique layout and vibe, so it's important to choose one that you are comfortable using.

When choosing a DAW, other factors to consider are:

- Compatibility: Make sure that the DAW is compatible with your computer's operating system.
- Features: Consider the features that are important to you, such as the number of audio tracks, the number of instrument tracks, and the types of effects and instruments that are included.
- Ease of use: Some DAWs have a steeper learning curve than others, so consider whether the DAW is easy for you to use.
- Price: DAWs can range in price from free to several hundred dollars, so consider how much you are willing to spend.

Some popular DAWs for synthwave music production include:

- Ableton Live: Ableton Live is a versatile DAW that is popular among electronic music producers. It features a unique session view that allows you to easily experiment with

different ideas and arrangements. It also includes a wide range of built-in effects and instruments.
- FL Studio: FL Studio is a popular DAW that is known for its user-friendly interface and powerful features. It includes a wide range of built-in instruments and effects, and it also supports VSTs and other third-party plugins.
- Logic Pro X: Logic Pro X is a professional-grade DAW that is used by many professional synthwave producers. It includes a wide range of built-in instruments and effects, as well as support for third-party plugins.

Once you have chosen a DAW, you will need to set it up. This typically involves installing the software on your computer and configuring your audio interface and MIDI controller. You will also need to set up your audio preferences, such as the sample rate and bit depth. You may also want to customize the layout and settings to suit your workflow.

It's also important to be familiar with the DAW you choose, you can do this by going through the tutorials and studying the manual that comes with the software. Additionally, there are many resources available online, such as YouTube tutorials and forums, that can help you learn how to use your DAW effectively.

2.2 Studio monitors

When setting up a home recording studio, one of the most important pieces of equipment you'll need is a set of studio monitor speakers. These are usually sold as single speakers, but you will need a pair for stereo playback. Cheaper sets are sometimes sold as pairs. Most modern studio monitors are "powered" speakers, meaning they have an internal amplification system that is designed for the speakers and cabinet. You will usually need a ¼" TRS to XLR cable to go from your audio interface's monitor outputs to the signal inputs of your speakers. Keep in mind that this *is not* the same cable as a regular ¼" jack to TRS. The proper connector will have an extra black ring as shown, making 3 separate metal connection points (this matches the 3-pronged XLR and is able to pass a 'balanced' line signal), as shown:

Balanced connector

*Suitable for connecting monitor outputs to powered speakers
*Balanced line connection

Unbalanced connector

*Suitable for connecting instruments
*unbalanced line connection
*not suitable for most studio monitors

Studio monitors are designed to provide a flat and accurate representation of the audio you're recording and mixing, unlike consumer speakers that are designed to enhance and color the sound. Choosing the right monitors for your studio can be a bit of a challenge, but with the right information, you'll be able to make an informed decision.

The first thing to consider when choosing studio monitors is the size of the speakers. The most common sizes are 5" and 8", and both have their own set of pros and cons. 5" monitors are compact and take up less space, which makes them perfect for small home studios or tight spaces. They're also less expensive than 8" monitors and are ideal for those on a budget. On the other hand, 8" monitors have a larger speaker and can handle more power, which means they can produce a louder and more accurate sound. They're also better suited for larger rooms and are ideal for professional studios.

Next, consider the type of music you'll be working on. If you're producing electronic or hip-hop music, you'll want monitors that can handle a wide frequency range, as these genres often have a lot of bass frequencies. On the other hand, if you're producing rock or country music, you'll want monitors that can handle a wide dynamic range, as these genres often have a lot of volume changes.

When it comes to specific models, the KRK Rokit series is a popular choice among home studio owners. They're available in both 5" and 8" sizes and are known for their accurate sound and affordable price. Another great option is the Kali Audio LP and IN series, which are known for their wide frequency range and accurate soundstage.

In addition to your monitors, you'll also need to consider your room's acoustics. A room with hard surfaces and parallel walls can cause reflections and standing waves, which can color the sound of your monitors. It's important to invest in some acoustic treatment such as bass traps, diffusers, and absorbers to ensure an accurate representation of your sound.

When choosing studio monitors for your home recording set-up, consider the size of the speakers, the type of music you'll be working on, and the acoustics of your room. It's also important to consider your budget, as prices can vary widely. With the right monitors and room treatment, you'll be able to produce high-quality and accurate music that sounds great on any playback system.

2.3 Using and installing Reaper

Although any DAW will suffice, for the rest of this book, we will be using Reaper as the DAW for our examples. This is because Reaper's ease of use, professional features, and the fact that it's controls are universal enough to be a generic example. There should be no problem following along even if you are using a different DAW, although you must be aware that the specific terminology used may be slightly different for your DAW.

Another reason I'm using Reaper as our example DAW is because it is very affordable at $60, and because it can actually be used free of charge. To clarify, Reaper costs $60. But you can use the "trial version" for free, indefinitely. The trial version is 100% full-featured, and never expires. There is literally no functional difference between the trial version and the paid version. Essentially this means you can use Reaper for free, for as long as you want. Because Reaper's payment is on "the honor system", I would highly recommend actually paying for it if you do decide to use it for an extended period of time.

Reaper's single drawback for producing synthwave is that it does not come with many (or any) suitable virtual instruments or synthesizers. I actually don't mind this, since I mostly use 3rd party plug-ins anyway. For those on a tight budget, I have also included a list of high quality free plug-ins and virtual instruments later in this chapter.

Here are instructions for getting Reaper up and running on your computer. You should also have an audio interface at this point to use in conjunction with your DAW software.

Reaper is a powerful and flexible digital audio workstation (DAW) software that can be used to record, edit, and mix audio. Here are step-by-step instructions on how to download, install, and set up Reaper with an audio interface:

Step 1: Download Reaper
- Go to the website (www.reaper.fm)
- Click on the "Download" button on the top left corner of the website
- Click on the "Download" button next to the appropriate version of Reaper
- Once the download is complete, run the installation file and follow the prompts to install Reaper on your computer.

Step 2: Set up Audio Interface and/or Install ASIO drivers
- If you have a brand-new audio interface, defer to the instructions that it came with. If you do not have specific instructions, refer to the following procedure.
- Connect your audio interface to your computer using a USB cable, and power the device on (if necessary).
- At this point, it may automatically begin downloading the appropriate drivers from the internet. If not, go to the website of the audio interface manufacturer and download the ASIO drivers for your device
- If necessary, run the installation file and follow the prompts to install the drivers on your computer
- Once the installation is complete, make sure your audio interface is selected in the Windows or macOS sound settings

Step 3: Set up Reaper
- Open Reaper
- Go to the "Options" menu and select "Preferences"
- In the "Device" tab, select your audio interface from the list of available devices

- In the "Audio" tab, select the ASIO driver for your audio interface
- Click "OK" to save the settings
- In the "Track" menu, select "Insert new track" to create a new audio track
- In the "Track" menu, select "Insert new track" to create a new audio track
- In the "I/O" section of the new track, make sure the input is set to your audio interface
- Make sure your audio interface is selected as the input and output device in the "Audio" tab of the preferences

Step 4: Test audio input and output
- Connect a microphone or instrument to the input of your audio interface
- In the new track, click the "Record enable" button to arm the track for recording
- Click the "Record" button in the transport bar to start recording
- Speak or play an instrument into the microphone or instrument connected to the audio interface
- Click the "Stop" button in the transport bar to stop recording
- Playback the recorded audio to ensure that the input and output are properly configured and working

It's important to note that the exact steps may vary depending on your specific audio interface, but the general process of downloading, installing and setting up Reaper should be similar. By following these steps, you should be able to successfully download, install and set up Reaper with an audio interface. Remember to check the manufacturer's website for the most up-to-date instructions and to always keep your software and drivers updated for optimal performance.

Choosing and setting up a DAW is an important step in setting up a home studio for producing synthwave music. Consider the factors that are important to you and choose a DAW that is compatible with your computer, has the features you need, and is easy for you to use. With the right DAW and a little bit of practice, you'll be well on your way to producing professional-sounding synthwave tracks.

2.4 Reaper basics

Reaper is a powerful and versatile digital audio workstation (DAW) that offers a wide range of tools and features for music recording, editing, and mixing.

Here is a list of some of Reaper's basic GUI controls, and where they appear in the main window:

1. Track control panel: This panel contains the main controls for adjusting the volume, panning, and other parameters of a track. It also includes buttons for enabling and disabling effects, soloing, and muting tracks.

2. Transport controls: These controls include buttons for starting, stopping, and rewinding playback, as well as for recording and looping.

3. Timeline: This is the main area where audio and MIDI clips are placed and edited.

4. Track list: This is the list of tracks in the project, including the track name, type, and status.

5. Toolbar: This is a row of buttons at the top of the screen that provides quick access to frequently used features, such as the pencil tool for editing MIDI notes and the scissors tool for cutting audio.

6. Mixer: This provides a visual representation of the levels and panning of all tracks in the project.

7. FX browser: This is where you can browse and add effects to tracks.

8. MIDI editor: This is a separate window that allows for detailed editing of MIDI notes and controller data.

9. Tempo and time signature: These controls allow you to adjust the tempo and time signature of the project.

10. Routing window: This window is opened by the routing button in the track control panel, and is where you can create aux sends, receives, sidechaining, and complex routing structures.

11. VST window: this is the window that corresponds to the effect that is selected in the FX browser. This is where you will find the control panel for your soft-synths and other virtual instruments.

12. MIDI track: track with MIDI information instead of an audio file.

13. Audio track: A track with an audio file (such as a .wav file).

14. Effect insert: A slot for a VST effect. You can drag and drop effects from one slot to another to quickly copy them.

15. Channel fader: This is the volume fader for each individual channel.

16. Master fader: This is the volume fader for the entire mix.

17. Cursor: This is the spot in the time that is currently selected. This is the point where the track will start once played. Left click anywhere on the timeline to move the cursor.

18. Pan knob: This knob affects a channels pan (spread) between the left and right stereo channels.

To make the most of Reaper, it's important to become familiar with the hotkeys and commands that can be used to navigate and control the software quickly and efficiently. Here is a detailed and easy-to-understand article that lists and describes some of the most common and useful hotkeys and commands for Reaper:

1. Transport controls: These hotkeys are used to control the playback and recording of audio in Reaper. The basic transport controls include play/pause (spacebar), record (R), stop (X), and loop (L).

2. Editing tools: These hotkeys are used to edit audio and MIDI in Reaper. Some common editing tools include cut (C), copy (ctrl + C), paste (ctrl + V), and undo (ctrl + Z).

3. Navigation: These hotkeys are used to navigate the Reaper interface and audio files. Some common navigation hotkeys include zoom in (ctrl + +), zoom out (ctrl + -), and go to beginning/end of track (home/end).

4. Selection tools: These hotkeys are used to select and manipulate audio and MIDI in Reaper. Some common selection tools include select all (ctrl + A), select none (ctrl + D), and select all items in time selection (ctrl + shift + A).

5. Mixing and routing: These hotkeys are used to control the mixing and routing of audio in Reaper. Some common mixing and routing hotkeys include solo (S), mute (M), and increase/decrease track volume (ctrl + up/down arrow).

6. Track and item management: These hotkeys are used to manage tracks and items in Reaper. Some common track and item management hotkeys include create new track (ctrl + T), delete track/item (delete), and move track/item up or down (ctrl + shift + up/down arrow).

7. Plug-in management: These hotkeys are used to manage plug-ins in Reaper. Some common plug-in management hotkeys include open/close plug-in window (ctrl + P), and bypass/enable plug-in (ctrl + shift + P)

8. Markers and regions: These hotkeys are used to work with markers and regions in Reaper. Some common markers and regions hotkeys include add marker/region (ctrl + shift + M), and navigate to next/previous marker/region (ctrl + ',' / ctrl + '.')

9. File management: These hotkeys are used to manage files in Reaper. Some common file management hotkeys include save (ctrl + S), save as (ctrl + shift + S), and open (ctrl + O).

Reaper offers a wide range of hotkeys and commands to help users navigate and control the software quickly and efficiently. By becoming familiar with the common hotkeys and commands, you can save time and improve your workflow. It's important to remember that you can also customize these hotkeys to your liking, in the Reaper's preferences.

2.5 Free Plug-ins

Now that we have our DAW installed, and before we go any further, here is a list of free plug-ins that you can use if needed. Reaper does have most of the basic plug-ins you will need pre-installed (effects like EQ, compressors, limiters, etc.). However, Reaper's stock effects can sometimes leave something to be desired, and at the very least their user interfaces aren't very pretty (not at all important to the sound, I know… butI suppose it matters to some people). The effects in Reaper will either have the Rea prefix (vst plug-ins), or the JS prefix (Jesusonic), and both categories contain extremely useful plug-ins. I tend to use the ReaEQ effect a lot, and is my standard go-to EQ for 95% of my EQ needs while recording.

If you are using a DAW other than Reaper, you may not need these at all. Other DAWs like Ableton or FL Studio operate on the selling point that they provide you with premium effects as part of their initial software bundle. Usually (as in the case of the two DAW's previously mentioned), they come with a variety of audio effects as well as virtual instruments. With that said, here are some free plug-ins that you might need or want to experiment with.

Youlean Loudness Meter
A free and accurate loudness meter that displays LUFS.
https://youlean.co/youlean-loudness-meter/

Limiter No.6
A free "all in one" mastering plug-in that is fully capable and features a compressor, limiter, High Frequency limiter, clipper, and final output gain. Its GUI is an emulation of classic hardware units with knobs and VU needles.
https://vladgsound.wordpress.com/plugins/limiter6/

TDR VOS SlickEQ
An all-purpose mixing and mastering EQ from Tokyo Dawn. Free and flavorful.
https://www.tokyodawn.net/tdr-vos-slickeq/

OrilRiver
A free, high quality algorithmic stereo reverb with a simple and intuitive GUI.
https://www.kvraudio.com/product/orilriver-by-denis-tihanov

Tal-Reverb-4
A free reverb plugin with an 80s character that can be used to create spacious and lush reverb effects in synthwave production.
https://tal-software.com/products/tal-reverb-4

2.6 Paid plug-ins

Of course, there is going to be the question of "what synthesizer plug-ins do I really want for synthwave music? And the truth is... the pros probably aren't using "free" plugins, at least not for a lot of things. Software synthesizers are one of those things (for the most part). Here is a list of some serious software synthesizers. Not all are expensive, per-se, but all are paid, 3rd party (meaning they do not come with a DAW) soft-synth options.

1. U-He DIVA
2. Omnisphere
3. Equator 2
4. Sylenth1
5. Serum
6. Massive X
7. FM8
8. Zebra 2
9. Avenger
10. Largo
11. Flashback (Beatskillz)
12. Synthwave Drums 2 (Beatskillz)

2.7 Hardware vs. Software Synthesizers

The debate between hardware and software synthesizers is another common one in the music production community. Hardware synthesizers are physical devices that you can touch and play, while software synthesizers are digital programs that run on a computer or mobile device. Both have their own unique set of advantages and disadvantages.

Hardware Synthesizers Pros:
- They have a tactile, hands-on interface that allows for more improvisation and experimentation in sound design.
- They are often considered to be more reliable and durable than software synthesizers.
- They have a lower latency, which means that the sound produced is closer to the time the musician plays a note.
- They can be used standalone, without the need for a computer or another device.

Hardware Synthesizers Cons:
- They are typically more expensive than software synthesizers.
- They can be less versatile and have fewer features than software synthesizers.
- They can be less portable and take up more physical space.
- They may not be compatible with all the software and devices available.

Software Synthesizers Pros:
- They have a wide range of sound-shaping options and can create complex and detailed sounds.
- They are often more affordable than hardware synthesizers.
- They are more versatile and have more features than hardware synthesizers.
- They can be used on different platforms, such as computers, tablets, or mobile devices.

Software Synthesizers Cons:
- They can have a sterile or artificial sound that is often considered less pleasing than the warm, organic sound of hardware synthesizers.
- They can be less intuitive to use, with a more complex interface.
- They can be more prone to malfunction or failure than hardware synthesizers.
- They can have a higher latency, which means that the sound produced takes longer to be heard after the musician plays a note.

Both hardware and software synthesizers have their own unique set of advantages and disadvantages. Hardware synthesizers offer a tactile and hands-on interface, a more reliable and durable build and a lower latency. On the other hand, software synthesizers offer a wide range of sound-shaping options, more versatility, and can run on different platforms. Ultimately, the choice between hardware and software synthesizers depends on the individual's preferences, needs, and budget.

It should be noted that Hardware synths do not necessarily equal analog synths. Hardware is, as the name implies, a physical synthesizer (either with, or without the traditional piano-style keyboard). While some hardware synths are indeed analog, many (if not more) are digital synthesizers in a physical package. Digital synthesis comes in many specific flavors like FM (frequency modulation), additive, subtractive, granular, physical modeling, etc., and they all have their unique sound and programmability.

You might be asking, what is actually the difference between analog and digital anyway? Without getting too technical, analog synths use actual electronic circuitry to directly create and alter an electronic signal into a musical timbre. This means actual transistors, capacitors, and resistors wired together on a circuit board, oscillating and filtering a signal which is then amplified. There is no computer code or software involved in this, and is more akin to the guts of an old-school radio or TV.

Digital is exactly the opposite. The sound is created with code in the digital realm using one of the previously mentioned methods. When the sound is output from the synthesizer is passes through a digital to analog (D/A) filter in order to translate the digital signal to an analog electronic audio output. The main difference here is that digital, owing its sound to code, never changes. It's rock solid, but some might say stale and predictable. Analog on the other hand, owes its sound to a chain of hundreds, if not thousands of individual little electronic components, from resistors to transistors and everything in between. These little components are not passing "ones and zeros", but are physically changing and shaping electricity into something audible. As such, different environmental factors like temperature or humidity can slightly affect the behavior of the thousands of individual components in an analog synth

2.8 MIDI controllers

USB vs. traditional MIDI controllers

MIDI controllers are electronic devices that can send MIDI (Musical Instrument Digital Interface) data to a computer or other device to control software instruments or other MIDI-enabled equipment. There are a variety of different types of MIDI controllers available, each with their own unique features and capabilities.

Firstly, it should be mentioned that there are two main types of MIDI controllers in the world: "USB" controllers, and traditional MIDI controllers. The difference between MIDI controllers that use USB and those that use a traditional MIDI connector is the way they connect to a computer. A MIDI controller that uses USB will connect directly to a computer via a USB cable, and the computer will recognize it as a standard USB device. This is the most common type of MIDI controller and it's the easiest to connect. They can also provide power to the controller, eliminating the need for an external power source.

On the other hand, you have the old-school of MIDI controllers that use a traditional MIDI connector. This will connect to a computer using the MIDI input on your audio interface (if it has one), or a separate MIDI-to-USB interface. The type of connection the MIDI protocol traditionally uses is a 5-pin DIN connector, which is not at all common on modern computers as is USB. This type of controller was designed with other MIDI gear in mind (not computers). In the 80s, when MIDI technology first became available, it was a way for different pieces of keyboard gear to communicate with each other. This is how older rack-mount synthesizers were able to be controlled by keyboard synths acting as a master controller.

Both types of MIDI controllers will work with most DAWs, but the USB MIDI controllers are generally more versatile since they are plug and play, and don't require additional hardware. USB MIDI controllers also can be compatible with iOS devices, and some models can even be powered by the device they are connected to. However this varies widely depending on the device, and the IOS generation you are trying to use with it. On the other hand, traditional MIDI controllers are more versatile in terms of physical connectivity (especially with older digital synths from the 80s and 90s), but they can be more complex to set up and use.

In short, USB MIDI controllers are more convenient and easy to set up, while traditional MIDI controllers provide a more versatile connectivity option, but require additional hardware.

Other types of MIDI controller

Here is a detailed overview of some other common types of MIDI controllers:

1. Keyboard controllers: These are the most common type of MIDI controllers and typically have piano-style keys. They can have a variety of different key counts, ranging from 25 to 88 keys, and can include features such as velocity sensitivity, aftertouch, and built-in arpeggiators. They are primarily designed for playing software instruments and can be used for a wide range of music genres.

2. Pad controllers: These MIDI controllers have a layout of velocity-sensitive pads, similar to those found on an MPC (Music Production Center) or drum machine. They are often used for triggering samples, drum sounds, and loops, and can also be used for playing software instruments.

3. Wind controllers: These are MIDI controllers that are played by blowing into them, similar to a wind instrument. They are often used by musicians who play woodwind or brass instruments and want to control software instruments with their breath controller.

4. DJ controllers: These MIDI controllers are specifically designed for DJs and electronic music producers. They typically include a variety of different controls such as jog wheels, faders, and knobs, and are used for controlling DJ software and performing live.

5. Guitar controllers: These are MIDI controllers that are designed to be played like a guitar, typically consisting of a fretboard and strings. They can be used to control software instruments, and also to control parameters in guitar effect pedals.

6. Foot Controllers: These are MIDI controllers that are played by the user's feet, typically using a set of pedals. They are often used to control effects and parameters during live performances, and can also be used to control software instruments.

7. Control Surface: These are MIDI controllers that are designed to control multiple parameters in a DAW or other software. They typically include a variety of knobs, faders, and buttons that can be assigned to control different parameters.

MIDI controllers come in a variety of different types and can be used for a wide range of music production and performance tasks. They range from keyboard controllers to pad controllers, DJ controllers, wind controllers, guitar controllers, foot controllers, and control surfaces. Each type of controller has its own unique features and capabilities

2.9 Supplemental info: What is a ROMpler?

A "rompler" is a type of electronic musical instrument that combines the functions of a sampler and a synthesizer. A sampler is an electronic instrument that allows a user to record and play back audio samples, while a synthesizer is an electronic instrument that generates sound through various means, such as oscillators, filters, and envelopes. A rompler combines these two functions by using pre-recorded samples as the basis for its sound generation, rather than generating sound from scratch like a traditional synthesizer.

A rompler typically has a library of samples that are stored on a built-in hard drive, CD-ROM, or flash memory. These samples can be played back and manipulated in various ways, such as changing the pitch, duration, or adding effects like reverb or delay. Additionally, a rompler can also have other features such as a built-in arpeggiator, drum machine, and sequencing capabilities.

Romplers often have a keyboard interface, but the term "rompler" isn't exclusively used for keyboard instruments, it can also refer to standalone rack-mountable units or even software instruments. They often have a wide range of sounds, from traditional instruments like pianos, drums, and guitars to more abstract and electronic sounds.

Some of the advantages of using a rompler include:

- Large sound libraries: Romplers often have a vast library of sounds that can be used right out of the box. This can save time and effort compared to creating sounds from scratch with a traditional synthesizer.
- Ease of use: Romplers are often simpler to use than traditional synthesizers, making them a good choice for musicians who are new to sound design and synthesis.
- Versatility: With a wide variety of sounds available, romplers can be used in a wide range of music styles and genres.

Some of the disadvantages of using a rompler include:

- Limited sound design capabilities: While romplers can be used to create a wide range of sounds, they are generally less flexible than traditional synthesizers when it comes to sound design.
- Lack of authenticity: Since romplers use pre-recorded samples, the sounds may not be as authentic as those produced by a traditional instrument.
- Limited sound manipulation capabilities: While it's possible to manipulate the sound of a rompler, the range of possibilities is often more limited than those of a traditional synthesizer.

A ROMpler is an electronic instrument that combines the functions of a sampler and a synthesizer. Romplers use pre-recorded samples as the basis for their sound generation and have a wide range of sounds and features that can be used right out of the box. It's a versatile instrument that can be used in a wide range of music styles and genres, but at the same time it has some limitations in terms of sound design capabilities and authenticity.

2.10 What synthesizer do I get?

A synthesizer is a crucial piece of equipment for producing synthwave music. A synthesizer allows you to create and manipulate sounds, which is essential for creating the retro, synth-heavy sound that defines the genre. When selecting and purchasing a synthesizer, there are a few things to consider:

1. Type of synthesizer: There are several different types of synthesizers available. We're already examined the analog vs. digital debate, but it is important to note that there are many more types of digital synthesis, such as subtractive, additive, sample-based, wavetable, FM, and others. It also bears repeating that being hardware-based does not necessarily mean analog, as many hardware synthesizers employ one of the digital synthesis engines previously mentioned. Analog synthesizers use analog circuitry to generate sound, while digital synthesizers use digital signal processing. So while digital synths can live in your computer or be a physical unit, analog synths have to be a physical unit by their very nature. Each type has its own unique sound and characteristics, so consider which type of synthesizer is best for your needs.

2. Features: Consider the features that are important to you, such as the number of oscillators, the types of filters, and the types of modulation options. Some synthesizers also include built-in effects, such as reverb and delay, which can be useful for creating a retro sound.

3. Price: Synthesizers can range in price from a few hundred dollars to several thousand dollars, so consider how much you are willing to spend.

4. Brand and model: Some brands and models are more popular among synthwave producers than others, such as Roland SH-101, Moog Minimoog, and Korg MS-20. Researching and trying out different brands and models can help you determine which one is the best fit for your needs and preferences.

5. Software synthesizers: In addition to hardware synthesizers, you can also use software synthesizers, such as Omnisphere, Serum, and Massive, which can be used in DAW. These software synthesizers can produce a wide range of sounds and have many advanced features, and they are often more affordable than hardware synthesizers.

Other necessary equipment for making synthwave music include a drum machine, an audio interface, and a MIDI controller. A drum machine is an electronic musical instrument that produces a variety of drum sounds. The Roland TR-808 and LinnDrum are popular choices among synthwave producers. An audio interface is used to connect your synthesizer, drum machine, and other pieces of equipment to your computer, and a MIDI controller is a device that allows you to control the parameters of your synthesizer and drum machine using knobs, sliders, or keys.

A synthesizer is a crucial piece of equipment for producing synthwave music, but it's not the only thing you need. A drum machine, an audio interface, and a MIDI controller are also necessary to make a complete synthwave setup. When selecting and purchasing equipment, consider the type of synthesizer, the features, the price, the brand and model, and also consider software synthesizers as an option. With the right equipment and a little bit of practice, you'll be able to create professional-sounding synthwave tracks from the comfort of your own home.

2.11 Free VST Synths and drums

If you're reading this and you don't have any synths (yet), this section is for you. I understand that hardware synths are very much a luxury, and software synths can be expensive. I also know that Reaper does not come with a full-stack of virtual instruments that are sufficient for making synthwave (like some other DAWs do), and this is a bit of a problem for many people. In order to remedy this, and to make synthwave production accessible to as many readers as possible, I've included a full list of absolutely free plug-ins. This list includes all the virtual instruments and soft-synthesizers that you will need to make professional level synthwave tracks. Also on the list are free effect plug-ins that cover compression, mastering, and other essentials.

Here is a list of some popular free VST plug-ins that are commonly used in synthwave production:

1. TAL-Noisemaker: A versatile synthesizer that emulates classic analog sounds and can be used to create a wide range of synthwave sounds.
    https://tal-software.com/products/tal-noisemaker

2. Tyrell N6: A software synthesizer that emulates the classic Roland SH-101 synthesizer and can be used to create vintage synthwave sounds.
    https://u-he.com/products/tyrelln6/

3. Synth1: A software synthesizer that emulates the classic Clavia Nord Lead 2 synthesizer and can be used to create a wide range of synthwave sounds.
    https://www.kvraudio.com/product/synth1-by-daichi-laboratory-ichiro-toda

4. SunVox: A modular synthesizer and sequencer that can be used to create a wide range of synthwave sounds.
    https://www.warmplace.ru/soft/sunvox/

5. Helm: A free, open-source, cross-platform synth that can be used to create a wide range of synthwave sounds.
https://tytel.org/helm/

6. Dexed: A free FM synthesizer that emulates the classic Yamaha DX7 synthesizer and can be used to create retro synthwave sounds.
https://www.kvraudio.com/product/dexed-by-digital-suburban

7. Sitala Drum: A free drum machine plugin that can be used to create classic and unique drum sounds in synthwave production.
https://decomposer.de/sitala/

8. DR-84: DR-84 is a virtual drum instrument that brings together the sounds of the most popular drum machines of the 80sl. From Pepto Audio. Highly recommended.
https://www.kvraudio.com/product/dr-84-by-pepto-audio

Please note that these are some of the popular free VSTs used in synthwave production, but it's not an exhaustive list and there are many more VSTs that can be used depending on the specific needs of the production.

2.12 Outboard preamps

To be honest, you really don't need an outboard preamp. Most audio interfaces available today have very good, clean, and clear onboard preamps, and these are perfectly capable of recording professional quality vocals (or any other audio you're trying to capture). Since most preamps (even the ones on cheaper interfaces) are perfectly fine, other things like microphones, and especially your singer and acoustic space will make a much bigger difference in the quality of your vocal recordings.

With that said, I thought I should add a bit about mic preamps since they are probably the most popular "secondary" purchase for new studio owners. If your music is very vocal-intensive, or you will be recording acoustic instruments and you want the absolute best fidelity– you might want to invest in a quality mic preamp. While they can certainly sound better, cleaner, and fitr a high-end microphone better than a stock preamp, you have to be careful that your interface is capable of bypassing its own onboard preamps. If not, then you will be feeding a high-end microphone preamp's "super clean" signal into a lower grade onboard preamp, which will then "color" the high end signal with its lower-quality artifacts, i.e. distortion, noise, etc. As you can see, this is hardly an improvement. In order to have the "high-end" signal pass directly into your interface, you need "line-level" inputs on your interface that bypass any kind of gain control and go directly to your interface's A/D (analog to digital) converter. This is not a feature that is found on every interface, so be sure before buying if this is something you are looking for.

Tube preamp

1/4" input in front, XLr in back
one knob (gain/volume)
simple design
the more you push it, the warmer it sounds

Solid state preamp

multiple impedance inputs
level selector knob
gain knob
VU meter
multiple impedance selections
headphone output

Image 2.12A

Image 2.12A shows two popular preamps in the under-$1000 price range. The one on top is the Blue Robbie ($999), and the one on the bottom is the Focusrite ISA One ($699). The Robbie is a tube preamp. It's powered by an EC88 tube, and has 34 dB of headroom gain (which isn't a lot, to be honest). It's an extremely simple design.

The ISA One is a solid state preamp, with a few more controls and a more complicated layout. It has a headphone output and separate headphone amp (with gain), which is an unusual feature. It also features various levels of gain and input impedance control. Overall, it allows you a much more precise level control, with more headroom gain, and an even cleaner signal. The details listed for each preamp is not necessarily typical or limited to that type of preamp. There are tube preamps with extensive controls, for instance.

2.13 Tips for creating a comfortable and efficient workspace

Creating a comfortable and efficient workspace in a home music studio environment is essential for producing quality music and staying motivated. Here are some tips for setting up your home music studio workspace:

1. Choose the right location: The location of your home music studio should be a quiet and distraction-free space. It should also be well-ventilated, with good lighting and a comfortable temperature.

2. Organize your equipment: Keep your equipment organized and easily accessible. This will save you time and make it easier to stay focused on your music. Use shelves, racks, and storage containers to keep your equipment in order.

3. Invest in a comfortable chair: You will be spending a lot of time sitting in your home music studio, so it's important to invest in a comfortable chair. A chair with good lumbar support will help to prevent back pain.

4. Minimize distractions: Keep your workspace free of distractions such as televisions, smartphones, and social media. Use noise-canceling headphones or earplugs to block out external sounds.

5. Create a comfortable environment: Make sure that your home music studio is comfortable and inviting. Consider adding plants, artwork, and other decorative elements to create a pleasant atmosphere.

6. Use a monitor stand: Using a monitor stand to elevate your computer screen to eye level will help to reduce neck and eye strain.

7. Have good lighting: Good lighting is important for staying focused and motivated. Consider using a combination of natural and artificial light to create a well-lit workspace.

8. Take regular breaks: It's important to take regular breaks to rest your eyes and stretch your legs. Use a timer to remind yourself to take a break every hour or so.

9. Have a clutter-free space: Keep your workspace free of clutter. A cluttered space can be overwhelming and make it difficult to focus.

10. Personalize it: Add personal touches to your workspace that will make you feel comfortable, such as a favorite poster, a picture of your loved ones, or a unique decoration.

Alway keep self-care in mind! By following these tips, you can create a comfortable and efficient workspace in your home music studio. This will help you to stay focused and motivated, so you can produce quality music and achieve your goals. Remember to take time to customize your studio to your preferences and you'll be more productive, motivated and inspired.

Part III: Music Theory and Composition

3.1 A word on composing music

Music composition, a.k.a. "Songwriting" is an extremely in-depth art in and of itself. For that reason, I'm not going to go too far into this subject. I debated if I should include this section, or if I should keep this book strictly within the realm of studio engineering. I thought I should include this section, even if it could have been omitted, or isn't something that you'd find in a typical "how to record music" book.

As previously stated, I won't be going too far into the details of how to actually compose. If you are already musically inclined, and have your compositions ready to go, or are ready to create them yourself now; you can skip over this entire chapter. Since I am going to assume that there will be readers with zero music and song-writing experience, I will give some very basic examples and instructions in this chapter. Please keep in mind, the music people want to compose is so extremely subjective, that it would do little good to spend time explaining details that might not be interesting for most readers. Because this book is meant primarily for beginners, I will give what I feel are good "starting point" examples of actual musical parts for various instruments and arrangements.

As a beginning musician/producer, I'm going to assume that you have certain musical artists that inspire you, and you are going to want to emulate. First of all, don't feel bad about this. Everyone has to start somewhere, and every big rockstar and musician started out looking up to other musicians (and trying to emulate them) just like you. If you have a certain musical artist in mind that you are inspired by, and want to learn from their compositions, there are certainly some strategies to accomplish this.

1. Study the chord progressions and melody lines: Analyze the chord progressions and melody lines to understand the song's harmonic structure. Look for recurring themes and patterns that give the song its unique character.

2. Analyze the instrumentation: Analyze the instruments used in the song, including the synth leads, arpeggios, pads, and drums. Look for any unique or interesting sounds or techniques used in the production.

3. Study the drum patterns: Analyze the drum patterns used in the song, including the kick and snare patterns, cymbal patterns, and fills. Look for any unique or interesting grooves used in the song.

4. Analyze the bass line: Analyze the bass line used in the song and consider how it interacts with the other elements of the song, such as the chord progressions, melody lines, and drum patterns.

5. Study the use of effects: Analyze the use of effects, such as reverb, delay, and chorus, and consider how they contribute to the overall sound and atmosphere of the song.

6. Study the song's structure: Analyze the song's structure, including the intro, verse, chorus, and outro. Look for any unique or interesting structures or forms used in the song.

7. Analyze the song's tempo: Analyze the song's tempo and consider how it contributes to the overall feel and energy of the song.

8. Analyze the song's dynamic range: Analyze the song's dynamic range, including the levels of the various elements and how they interact with each other. Consider how this contributes to the overall balance and impact of the song.

Ideally, you are going to want to study and emulate as many songs, musicians, and musical styles as possible. Doing this is how we as humans "synthesize" our own unique artistic and musical styles. Nothing is created in a vacuum, and we are all an amalgamation of our individual past education and experiences.

3.2 The Piano Roll

We might as well start our journey into theory and composition with the DAW window that most facilitates this, the piano roll. As a synthwave musician, you will become very familiar with the piano roll. **The piano roll in Reaper is the MIDI editor window.**

A piano roll grid is a visual representation of a musical sequence, typically used in Digital Audio Workstations (DAWs) and electronic music production software. It is a two-dimensional grid that is divided into horizontal and vertical lines, representing time and pitch respectively. The horizontal axis represents the timeline of the sequence, and the vertical axis represents the pitch of the notes. Notes can be added to the grid by clicking on the corresponding point on the grid.

In relation to basic music theory, the piano roll grid can be used to visually represent the pitch and timing of notes in a melody, chord progression, or drum pattern. The vertical lines on the grid represent the different pitches of the notes, with the notes on the bottom of the grid being the lower pitches and the notes on the top of the grid being the higher pitches. The horizontal lines on the grid represent the timing of the notes, with the notes on the left of the grid being earlier in time and the notes on the right of the grid being later in time.

The piano roll grid also allows for the easy manipulation and editing of notes, such as changing their pitch, duration, and velocity. This allows for easy experimentation with different melodies, chord progressions, and drum patterns, and can be a useful tool for learning and understanding basic music theory concepts such as scales, chords, and timing.

Additionally, the piano roll grid also allows for the easy representation of different time signatures and different grid divisions, like 16th, 32nd, and 64th notes, it also allows for the representation of notes beyond the piano range, commonly used with electronic instruments, it can also be used to create unconventional rhythms and time signatures.

The piano roll grid is a useful tool in electronic music production and DAWs, it provides a visual representation of a musical sequence and it's relation to basic music theory, it can be used to create, edit, and experiment with different melodies, chord progressions and drum patterns, it allows for easy manipulation and editing of notes, and it can be used to represent different time signatures, grid divisions and unconventional rhythms.

3.3 Intervals and chords

Intervals are the distance between two notes in a musical scale. They are measured by counting the number of scale degrees between the two notes. Explained simply; Starting with the root note, you sequentially give each note in a given scale a number. Those numbers are now your "intervals". For example, in the scale of C major (C D E F G A B), C is your root note, and D is your 2nd interval. Staying in C major, E would be your 3rd interval..

It should also be noted that intervals are also classified according to their quality, which describes the relative size of the interval. For example, an interval between two notes that is the same size as a minor second interval, but is a half-step larger, is considered a major second interval. Similarly, intervals can be classified as perfect, major, minor, augmented, and diminished.

To describe another way; going back to our original example, we used the C major scale, and E is our 3rd interval. If we use the C minor scale (C D D# F G A B), then our third interval now changes to D#. This is because the interval is dependent on what scale is being used. This is how intervals can be used to describe a specific harmonic relationship such as major 3rd, minor 3rd, etc.

For now, the main thing to remember is that intervals are the distance between two notes in a musical scale, and they are measured by counting the scale degrees between them. For extra points, also know that intervals are classified by their size and quality, which helps to understand how they sound and how they are used in music. Understanding intervals is an important concept in music theory and is as fundamental as it gets. Keep intervals in mind as they come into play considerably in this chapter.

What is a chord?

A chord is a collection of two or more musical notes that are played or sung together to form a harmonious sound. It is the basic building block of harmony and is an essential part of music composition and theory. Chords can be made up of different types of intervals, such as major or minor, and can be played in various positions, such as root position, inversion, or extension. The choice of chords and the way they are used contribute to the overall musical style and emotion of a composition.

A chord is usually a group of three or more notes played simultaneously. Some basic chords can be built using relative intervals, which are the distances between the notes in the chord. Here are some examples of basic chords using relative intervals:

1. Major chord: The major chord is built from the root note, a major third interval, and a perfect fifth interval. For example, a C major chord is built from the notes C, E, and G.

2. Minor chord: The minor chord is built from the root note, a minor third interval, and a perfect fifth interval. For example, an A minor chord is built from the notes A, C, and E.

3. Diminished chord: The diminished chord is built from the root note, a minor third interval, and a diminished fifth interval. For example, a B diminished chord is built from the notes B, D, and F.

4. Augmented chord: The augmented chord is built from the root note, a major third interval, and an augmented fifth interval. For example, a G augmented chord is built from the notes G, B, and D#.

3.4 Basic music theory and chord progressions

Music theory and chord progressions are important concepts to understand when producing synthwave music. Basic music theory will help you to understand the building blocks of music and how to create melodies and harmonies that are pleasing to the ear. Chord progressions are the sequences of chords that are used in a song, and they can have a big impact on the overall feel and emotion of the music.

Music theory is a vast subject, but some basic concepts to understand include:
- Pitch: Pitch refers to the highness or lowness of a sound, and it is measured in hertz (Hz).
- Scales: A scale is a series of pitches arranged in ascending or descending order. The most commonly used scale in Western music is the major scale, which consists of seven pitches.
- Chords: A chord is a combination of two or more pitches played at the same time. The most basic chords are triads, which consist of three pitches.

- Intervals: As explained earlier, an interval is the distance between two pitches. Intervals can be measured in semitones (half-steps) or whole tones (whole-steps).
- Time signature: Time signature is the notation that tells us the number of beats in a measure and the type of note that represents one beat. Typical pop, dance, and electronic music utilizes a 4/4 time signature, which we will also use for our example.

The chords in our examples will be written as intervals (remember those?), which are notated in the form of Roman numerals. So for example, a "1, 4, 5" chord progression (where the root note is considered the "1") will be written as I-IV-V.

Rather than randomly pairing chords in hopes of finding something that sounds good, you can actually use chords that are within the same key for better harmonic coherence. This essentially means that you are composing with chords that compliment each other, rather than chords that sound awful together. For this example, we will stick to the key of C. In the key of C, we have the following chords:

- I = C Major.
- ii = D minor.
- iii = E minor.
- IV = F Major.
- V = G Major.
- VI = A Minor.
- vii° = B diminished.

When it comes to chord progressions, synthwave music often uses a combination of major and minor chords to create a retro and nostalgic feel. Some common chord progressions used in synthwave include:

- I-IV-V: This chord progression uses the first, fourth, and fifth chords of a major scale. It creates a sense of progression and movement and is often used in upbeat and energetic tracks. In the key of C major, these would be the C(i), F(iv), and G(v) chords.

- ii-V-I: This chord progression uses the second, fifth, and first chords of a major scale. It creates a sense of tension and release and is often used in more melodic and contemplative tracks. In the key of C major, these chords would be Dm7 (ii), G7 (V), and Cmaj7 (i)

- iii-vi-ii-V: This chord progression uses the third, sixth, and second chords of a major scale. It creates a sense of nostalgia and longing and is often used in more melancholic and nostalgic tracks. In the key of C, these chords would be Em7(iii), Am7(vi), Dm7(ii), G7(v)

It's also important to understand the use of chord inversions, which can make the progression sound more interesting, and add a sense of movement to the music. Using different voicings of chords can also add depth and interest to your music.

Understanding basic music theory and chord progressions is important for producing synthwave music. Basic concepts such as pitch, scales, chords, intervals, and time signatures can help you to create melodies and harmonies that are pleasing to the ear. Chord progressions, in particular, can have a big impact on the overall feel and emotion of the music. Experimenting with different chord progressions and voicings can help you to create unique and interesting tracks.

3.5 Song Key and Mood

If you wish to venture beyond the key of C, different song keys will evoke a different feel or emotion. Here is a list of song song keys from A to G#, along with the mood or feel that corresponds to it.

Here is a list of song keys, from A to G#, along with the corresponding mood or feel:

Key	Mood/Feel
A	Bright and uplifting
A#	Eerie and otherworldly
B	Majestic and grandiose
C	Calm and serene
C#	Dark and mysterious
D	Melancholic and introspective
D#	Intense and dramatic

E	Euphoric and triumphant
F	Relaxed and laid-back
F#	Tense and anxious
G	Nostalgic and longing
G#	Powerful and driving

It's worth noting that the mood or feel that corresponds to each key is subjective and can vary depending on context, listener, and also the tone or chord progression used in the song. Some keys can be used for different purposes, for example, a key like C# can evoke a dark and mysterious mood, but it can also be used to create a happy and upbeat feeling. In general, the key of a song is one of the many elements that contribute to the overall mood or feeling of a piece of music, and it's important to consider the other elements such as melody, harmony, rhythm and lyrics when interpreting the song.

3.6 Composing a Drum Beat

In this section, we aren't going to be going through the rhythm creation process step-by-step (we'll do that later, in the "tracking" section). Instead, we're going to talk about what makes a good drum or percussion part.

1. Retro Electro: This approach towards synthwave drums is heavily influenced by the drum sounds and patterns of the 1980s. The drums are often processed to sound like they were recorded on vintage hardware and have a distinct analog character. Examples of common synthwave drum beats in this style include the use of a Roland TR-808 or TR-909 drum machine, with a focus on snappy, tight snare drums, and deep, punchy kick drums. Examples of songs that use this style include "Nightcall" by Kavinsky and "The Grid" by Daft Punk.

2. New Wave: This approach towards synthwave drums is heavily influenced by the drum sounds and patterns of new wave and post-punk music from the 1980s. The drums often have a more minimalistic and experimental feel, with a focus on sparse, open hi-hat patterns and use of snare drums for emphasis. Examples of common synthwave drum beats in this style include the use of a Roland TR-808 or TR-909 drum machine, with a

focus on snappy, tight snare drums, and deep, punchy kick drums. Examples of songs that use this style include "Deadlines" by Com Truise and "Waves" by The Midnight.

3. Futuristic: This approach towards synthwave drums is heavily influenced by science fiction and futuristic themes. The drums often have a more mechanical and robotic feel, with a focus on precise, tight and fast 16th note hi-hat patterns and use of snare drums for emphasis. Examples of common synthwave drum beats in this style include the use of a Roland TR-808 or TR-909 drum machine, with a focus on snappy, tight snare drums, and deep, punchy kick drums. Examples of songs that use this style include "Echoes" by Lazerhawk and "The Chase" by Mitch Murder.

4. Fusion: This approach towards synthwave drums is heavily influenced by the fusion of different genres. The drums often have a more fusion of the 80s retro and the present, with a focus on tight and fast 16th note hi-hat patterns and use of snare drums for emphasis. Examples of common synthwave drum beats in this style include the use of a Roland TR-808 or TR-909 drum machine, with a focus on snappy, tight snare drums, and deep, punchy kick drums. Examples of songs that use this style include "Fury" by Timecop1983 and "Fading" by Mitch Murder.

Let's build

Let's talk some more about drum beats. A simple 4/4, 4-bar, 16th note drum pattern with a kick on beat one, a snare on beat four, and a 16th note closed hi-hat pattern is a common foundation for many electronic and synthwave productions. Here is a step-by-step explanation of how to create such a pattern, and the theory behind each part:

1. To notate this pattern, you would use standard drum notation. The kick drum would be notated with a bass drum note, typically a large "O" symbol. The snare drum would be notated with a snare drum note, typically a smaller "o" symbol. The closed hi-hat would be notated with an "x" symbol.

2. The kick drum is typically placed on the first beat of the measure, also known as beat one. This gives the pattern its strong backbeat and solid foundation. The snare drum is typically placed on beat three, giving the pattern a strong sense of forward motion and accenting the backbeat.

3. The closed hi-hat pattern is made up of 16th notes and is typically placed on beats 2 and 4 in each measure. This gives the pattern a sense of rhythm and movement. This pattern can be played in multiple ways, it can be swung or straight, it can be played with the foot or with the hand, the possibilities are endless.

4. Each rhythmic part of the pattern interacts musically to create the overall feel and groove of the pattern. The kick drum provides the foundation and backbeat, the snare drum

accentuates the backbeat and adds forward motion, and the closed hi-hat pattern adds a sense of rhythm and movement. Together, these elements create a cohesive and driving drum pattern that is suitable for many different styles of music.

A basic 4/4, four-bar, rock drum beat with a 16th note drum pattern that uses a kick on beat one, a snare on beat four, and a 16th note closed hi-hat pattern is a common foundation for many rock genres. Here is a step-by-step explanation of how this pattern would be counted and how each drum layer stacks and syncopates together:

1. To count this pattern, you would use standard drum notation counting. The kick drum would be counted on the "ONE" of each measure. The snare drum would be counted on the "FOUR" of each measure. The closed hi-hat pattern would be counted using the 16th note subdivisions. It would be counted as "ONE-e-and-uh - TWO-e-and-uh - THREE-e-and-uh - FOUR-e-and-uh" and so on.

2. The kick drum is typically placed on the first beat of the measure, also known as beat one. This gives the pattern its strong backbeat and solid foundation. The snare drum is typically placed on beat four, giving the pattern a strong sense of forward motion and accenting the backbeat.

3. The closed hi-hat pattern is made up of 16th notes and is typically placed on beats 2 and 4 of each measure. This gives the pattern a sense of rhythm and movement. This is played in a consistent pattern, usually the closed hi-hat is played on every 16th note.

4. Each rhythmic part of the pattern interacts musically to create the overall feel and groove of the pattern. The kick drum provides the foundation and backbeat, the snare drum accentuates the backbeat and adds forward motion, and the closed hi-hat pattern adds a sense of rhythm and movement. Together, these elements create a cohesive and driving drum pattern that is suitable for many different styles of rock music.

2.4.47   7

ONE-eee-and-uhh-TWO-eee-and-uhh-THR-eee-and-uhh-FOR-eee-and-uhh

1.2   1.3   1.4   2

C3

C2

Pay close attention to this!!!

There are 4 main beats

C1

C0

Each main beat is divided into 4 notes (one-ee-and-uh)
These are 16th notes. This is also your basic synth-bass rhythm

The four note beat repeats here

•Velocity

1

arp-a11   arp-a11.mid
bass-a11   bass-a11.mid

Grid: 1/16   ∨   straight ∨   Notes: Grid ∨   ☐ Key snap   Color: Velocity ∨

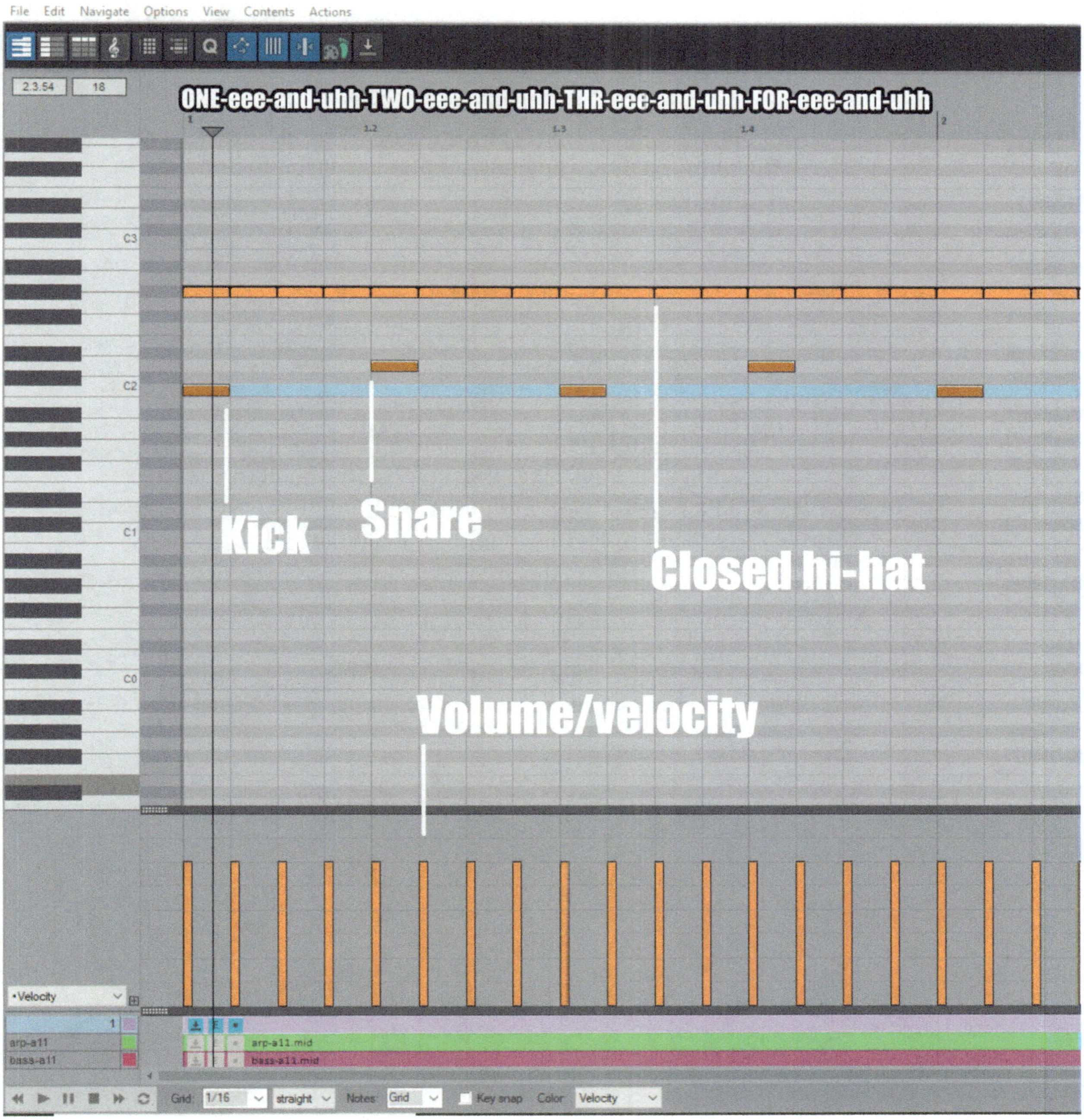
File Edit Navigate Options View Contents Actions
ONE-eee-and-uhh-TWO-eee-and-uhh-THR-eee-and-uhh-FOR-eee-and-uhh
Kick
Snare
Closed hi-hat
Volume/velocity
C3
C2
C1
C0
Velocity
arp-a11
bass-a11
arp-a11.mid
bass-a11.mid
Grid: 1/16 straight Notes: Grid Key snap Color: Velocity

Image 3.6B

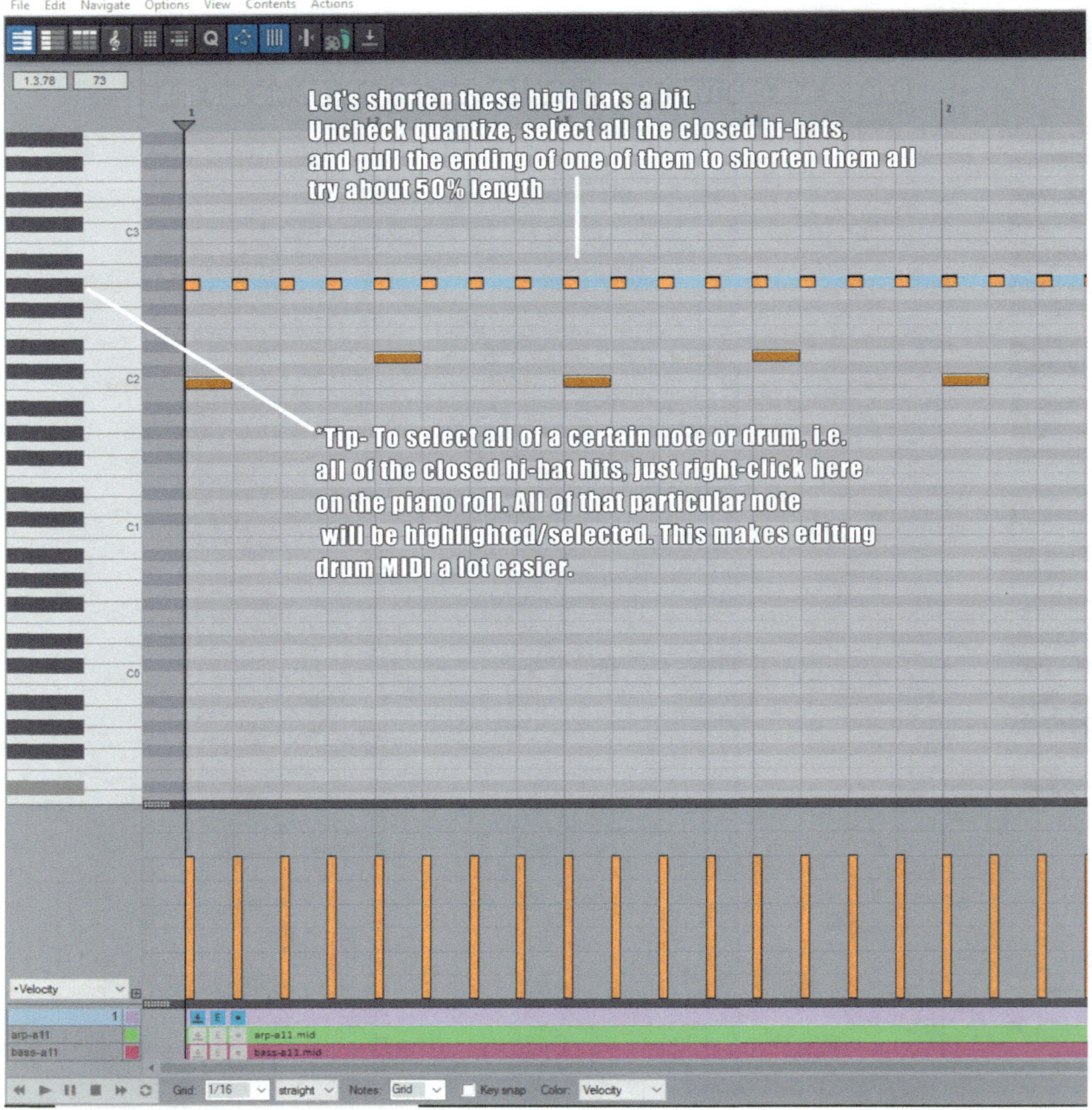

Image 3.6C

[Let's shorten these high hats a bit. Uncheck "snap-to", and select all the closed hi-hats, and pull the ending of one of them to shorten them all. Try about 50% length.]

[Tip- To select all of a certain note or drum, i.e. all of the closed hi-hats, just right-click on its corresponding note on the piano roll. All of that particular note will be highlighted/selected. This makes editing drum MIDI (or any MIDI) a lot easier.]

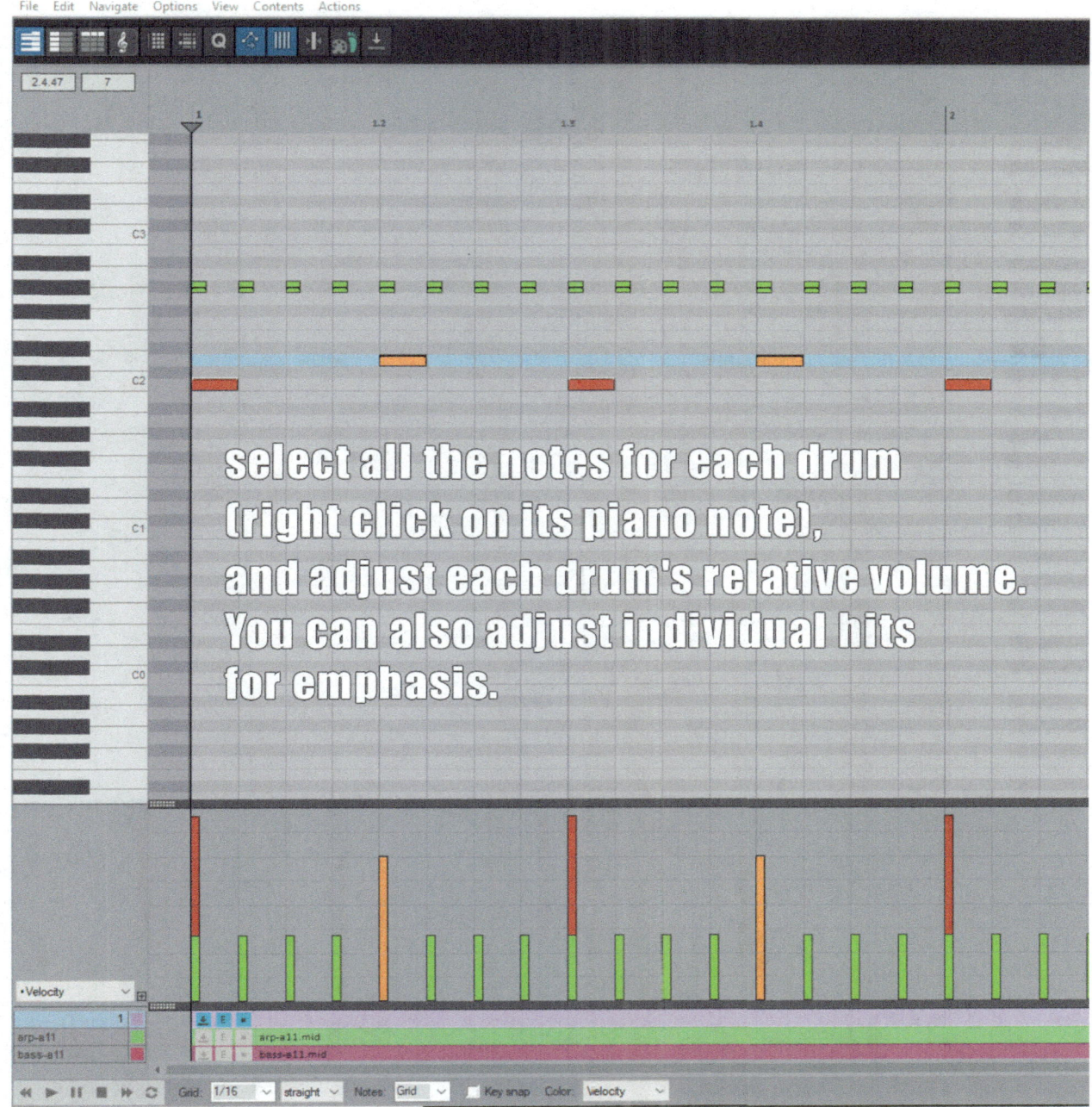

Image 3.6D

[Select all the notes for each drum (right click on its piano note), and adjust each drum's relative volume. You can also adjust individual hits for emphasis.]

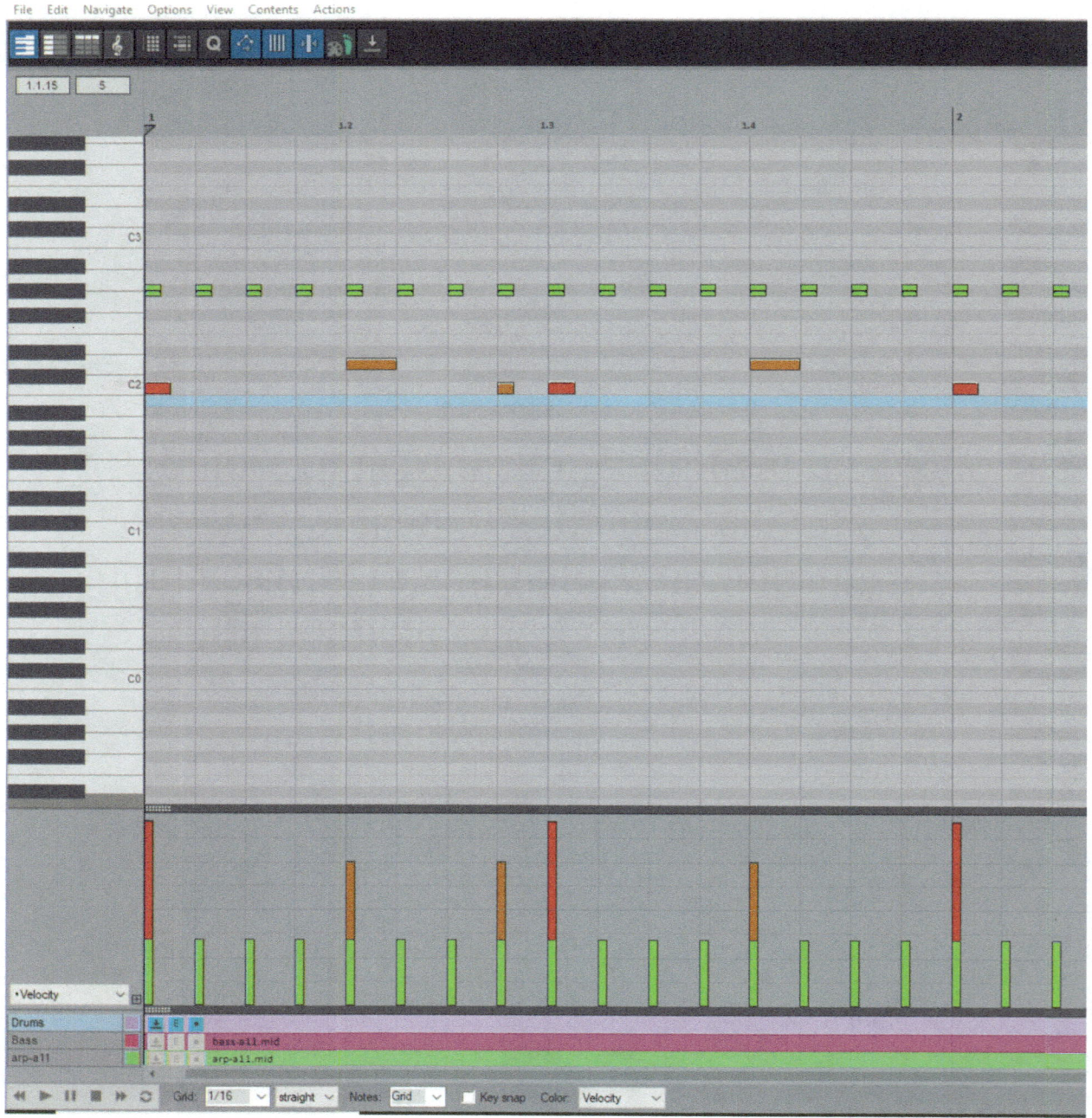

Image 3.6E

This is the same drum beat, but with a slight "pickup" accent on the first and third beat (the kick drum).

The following are a few more examples of various drum beats and fills.

Image 3.6F

This is a syncopated kick drum pattern. The kick lands on the "1" beat, but NOT the "3", as this is a syncopated kick drum. You can syncopate any drum.

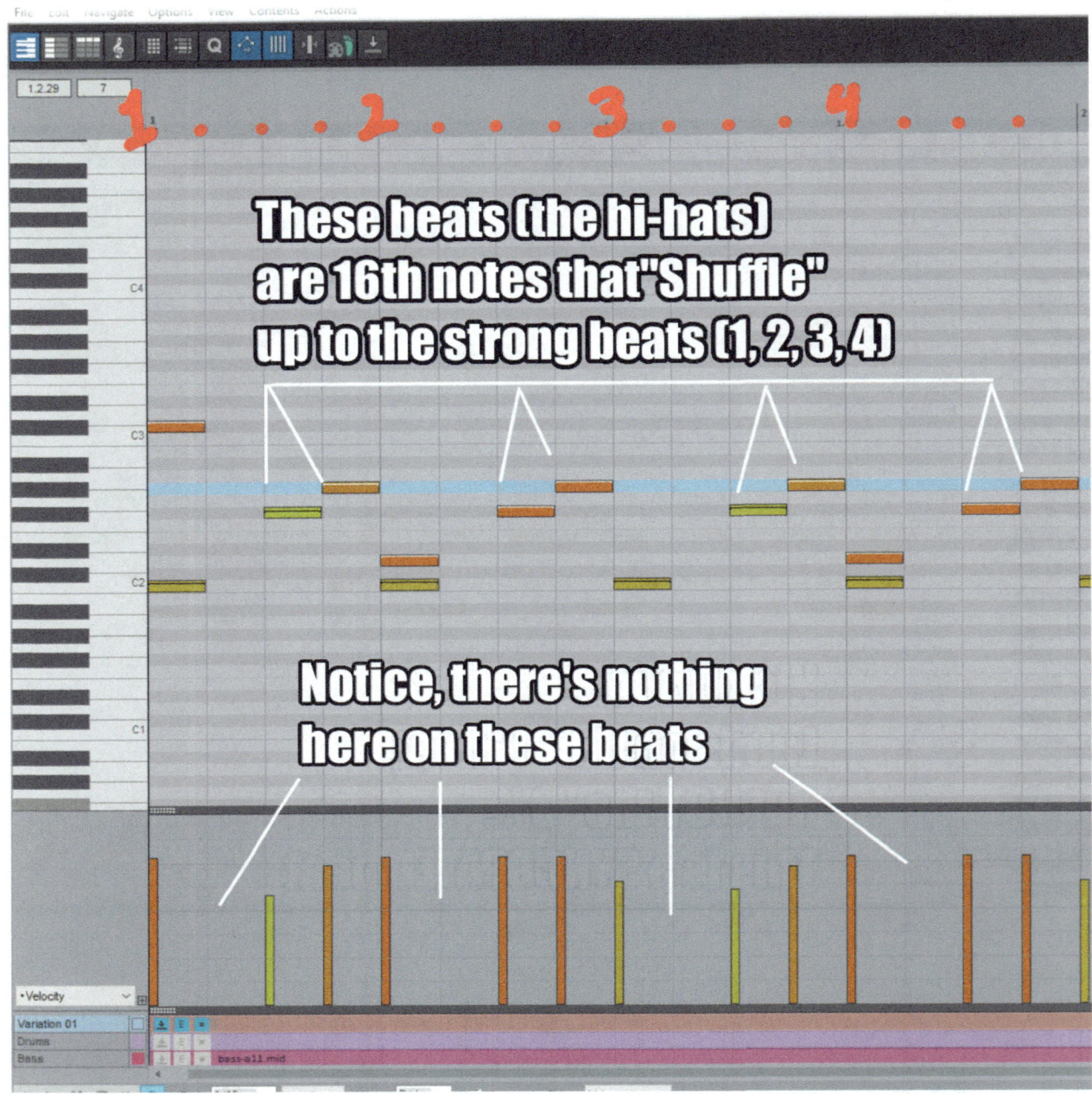

Image 3.6G

This is a 16th note "shuffle". It's not a real shuffle, but it sounds kind of like one even with heavy quantization. In this example, the two beats (a closing high hat followed by a closed high hat hit) are two 16th notes that "shuffle up" to the strong beats, namely the 1, 2, 3, and 4 beats. Notice that there is nothing on the 16th note right before the high hats. This empty space is necessary to create the "shuffle" effect. You can also shuffle different drum sounds, or even your bass rhythm.

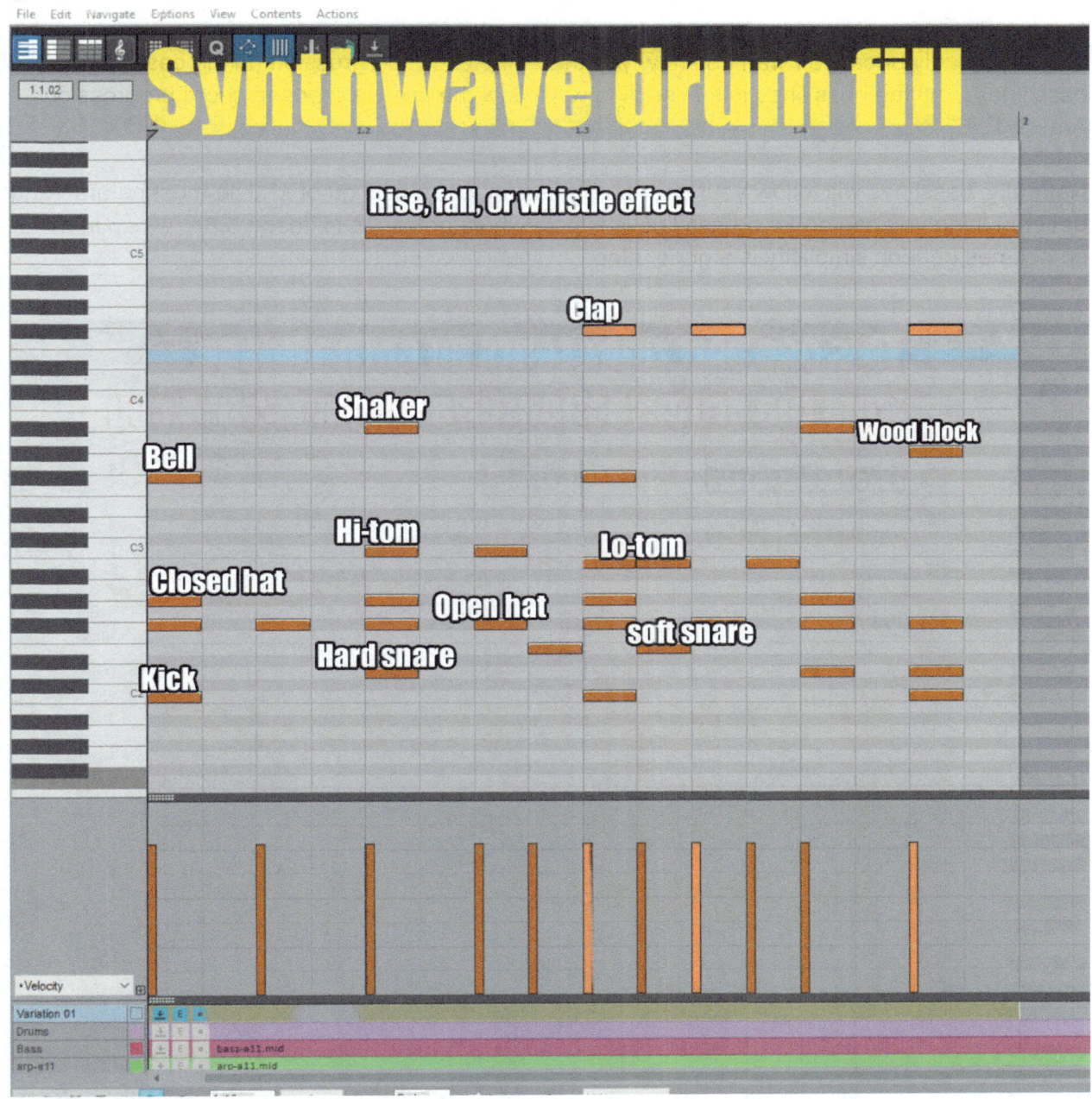

Image 3.6H

This is a typical **synthwave-styled drum fill** that would be found in the last four beats of a section. Notice that the overall part is generally busy with many different drums, but each individual drum is playing a relatively simple pattern.

3.7 Composing a bass line

Our bassline examples are going to be four times the length of our images of drum sequences. This is primarily because I want to show you the entire chord progression (in the case of the bass lines). All the bass lines in this section will follow the same supposed chord progression Am, G, F, E.

Naturally, basslines will follow your chord progression, or be built off of it. The most natural (and generic) thing you can do for a bass line is simple whole notes, as in image 3.6A. Keep in mind, sometimes generic simplicity is a good thing.

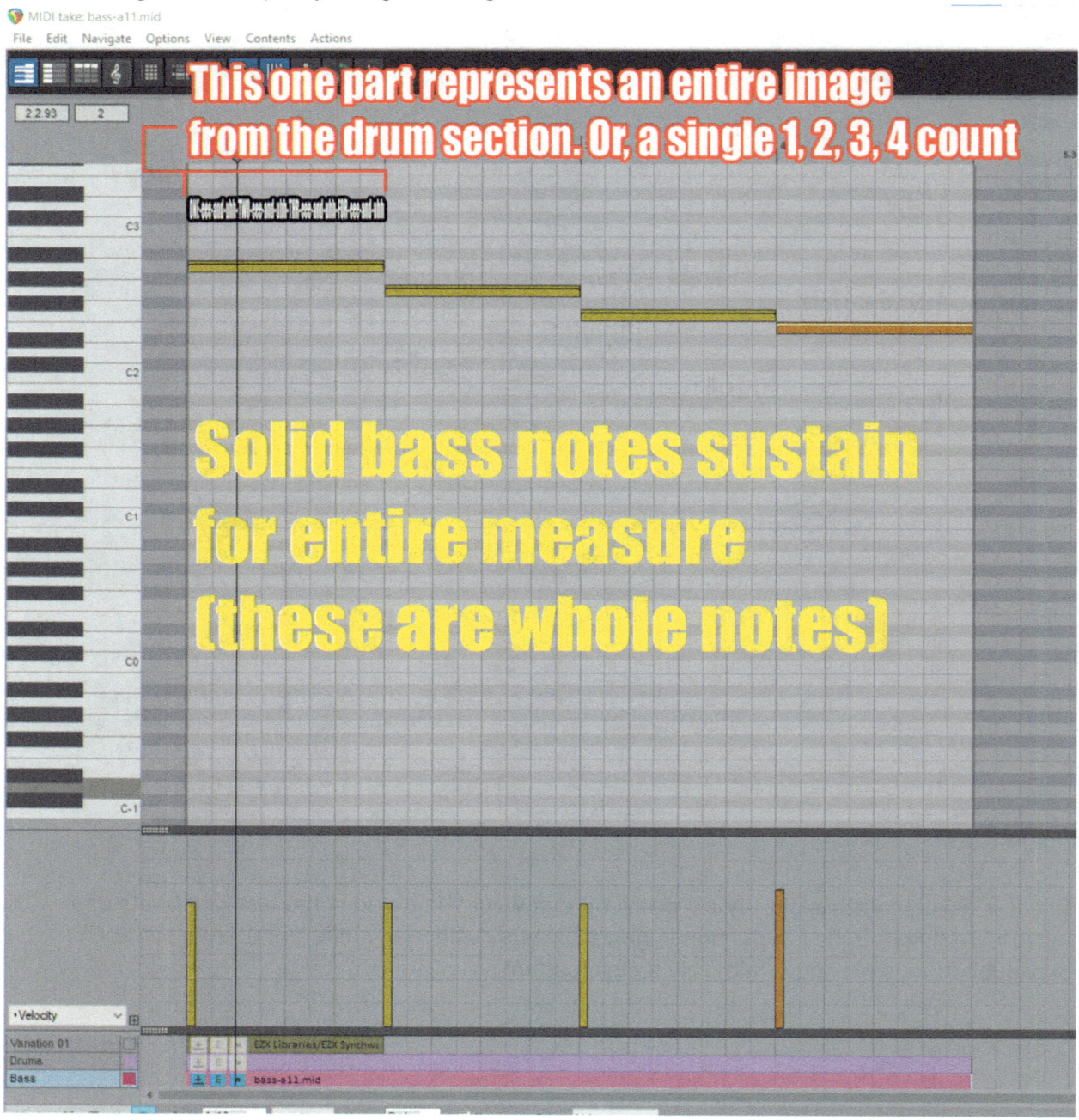

Image 3.7A

Contrary to following the chord progression exactly, you can also have a bassline that uses a "pedal" note, or inverts a chord. The first example is seen in image 3.6B, where we see an inverted bassline. Inverted means that the bassline does note follow the root note of the underlying chord.

Image 3.7B

As also mentioned, we've got what is a "pedal note" bassline. This is illustrated in image 3.6C. The pedal bassline stays on an underlying note that provides some harmonic tension against the chord progression. The pedal bass note stays constant while the chords change over it.

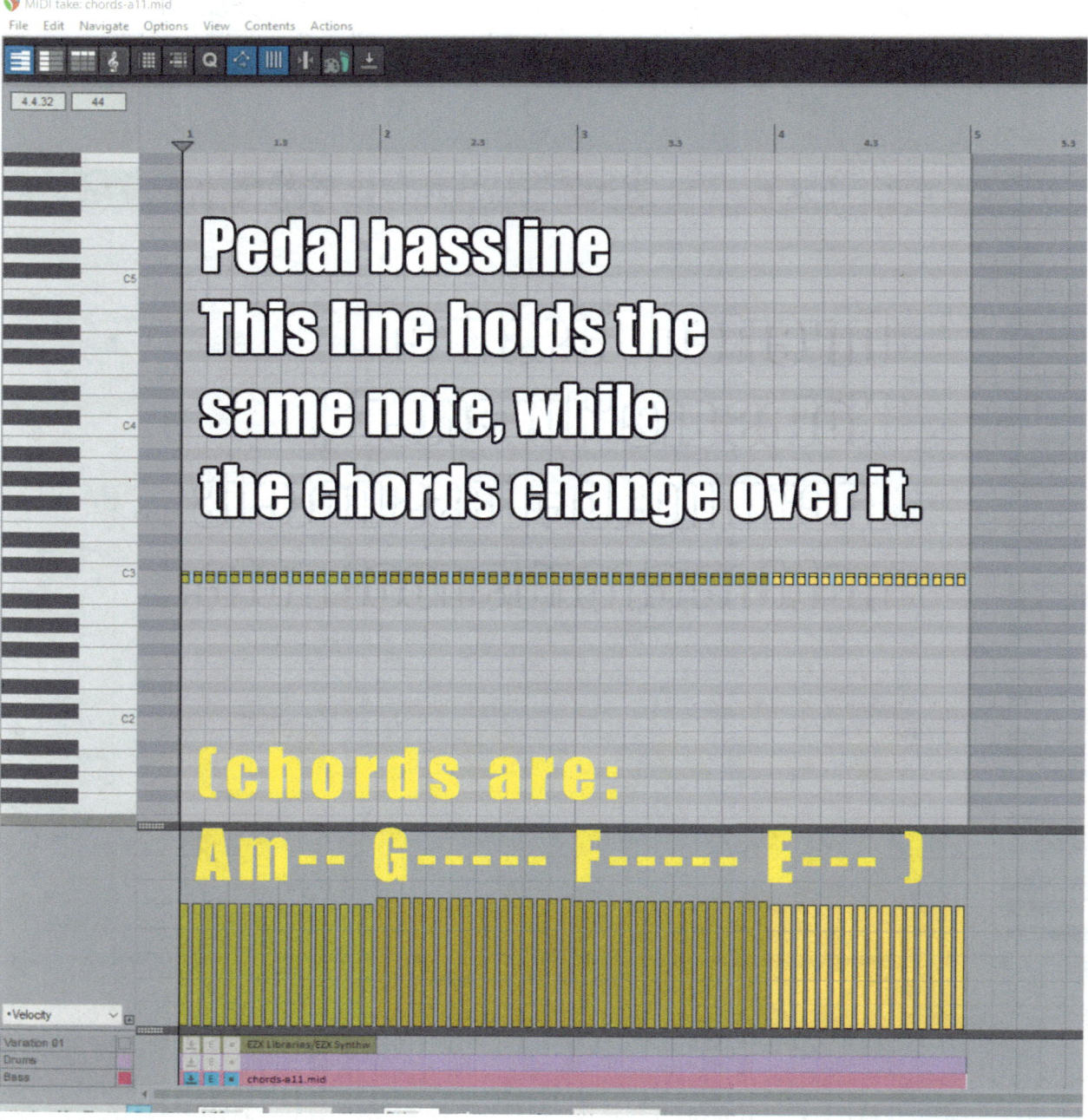

Image 3.7C

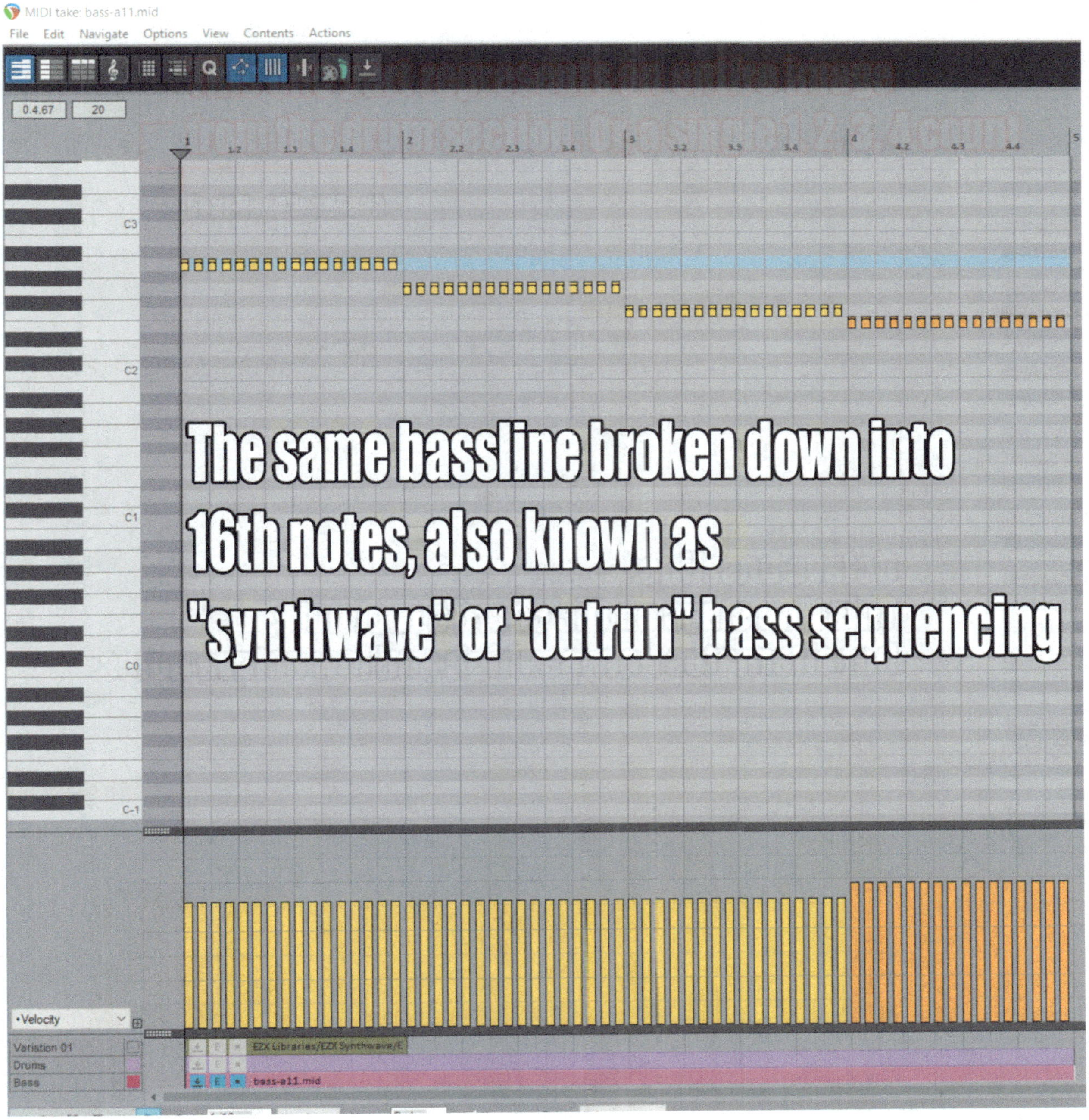

Image 3.7D

The "Synthwave Bassline" is seen in image 3.6D. A classic synthwave bass pattern that is characterized by a simple and repetitive 16th note pattern. The bassline is usually syncopated and is often played on a sawtooth or square wave synth sound.

Image 3.7E

Shown in image 3.6E is the octave bassline. This bassline typically stays on the chord's root note (or not), and alternates between a high and low octave of the same note. A popular carry-over from 70's disco music.

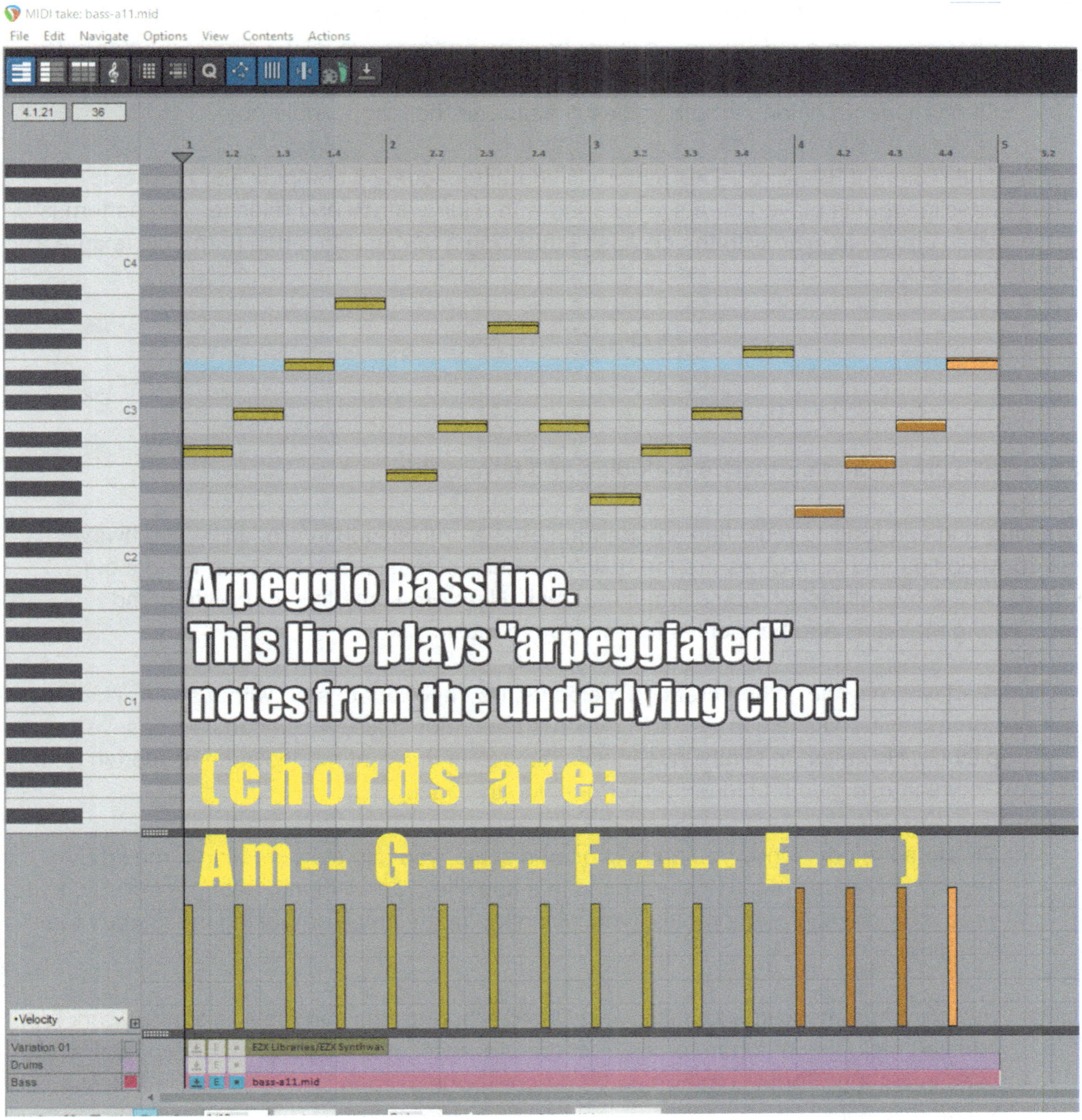

Image 3.7F

Lastly, we've got the "arpeggio" bassline in image 3.6F. The "Arpeggiated Bassline": This pattern is characterized by a fast arpeggiated pattern that is played on a synth sound with a short attack and release. The pattern is often syncopated and can create a sense of movement and energy in the track.

Some other examples of typical synthwave bass lines are:

1. The "Sub Bass": This pattern is characterized by a deep and powerful bassline that is often played on a sine wave synth sound. The pattern is usually a simple quarter note pattern and is used to add depth and power to the lower end of the frequency spectrum. Often made up of longer note values like quarter, half, and whole notes.

2. The "Chordal Bassline": This pattern is characterized by a complex and harmonic bassline that is played on a synth sound with a long attack and release. The pattern is often played in sync with the chords of the song and can add a rich harmonic texture to the track.

3.8 How to create and sequence melodies and harmonies

Creating and sequencing melodies and harmonies is a crucial step in producing synthwave music. Melodies and harmonies are the building blocks of music, and they can have a big impact on the overall feel and emotion of the track. Here are some tips for creating and sequencing melodies and harmonies for synthwave music:

1. Start with a scale: When creating melodies, it's important to start with a scale. The most commonly used scale in Western music is the major scale, which consists of seven pitches. However, in synthwave music, the use of different modes such as Dorian and Phrygian can give a unique and retro feel to the track.

2. Create a melody: Once you have chosen a scale, you can start creating a melody. A melody is a series of pitches arranged in a specific order. When creating a melody, try to keep it simple and memorable. Avoid using too many notes or making the melody too complex.

3. Use chord progressions to guide you: Chord progressions can provide a framework for creating melodies and harmonies. A chord progression is a sequence of chords that are used in a song. Some common chord progressions used in synthwave include I-IV-V, ii-V-I, and iii-vi-ii-V.

4. Experiment with chord inversions: Chord inversions can add depth and interest to your melodies and harmonies. A chord inversion is when the order of the notes in a chord is changed. For example, a C major chord is made up of the notes C, E, G. An inversion of the C major chord would be E, G, C.

5. Add harmony: Once you have created a melody, you can add harmony to it. Harmony refers to the combination of two or more pitches played at the same time. When adding harmony, try to use chords that complement the melody.

6. Experiment with different sounds. Believe it or not, timbre can inspire melody. Try a radically different timbre, i.e. a different synth patch or guitar tone, and you might just "hear" a melody that lends itself to that particular attack, tone, and amplitude. If you're searching for inspiration, I would recommend trying a sound that's radically different from what you're currently using (and bored with). If you're striking out while using a harsh sound with an immediate attack, like a super saw or distorted guitar, try switching over to a mellower sound like a choir, or swell pad. The difference in timbre may give you immediate inspiration in a direction that you haven't looked towards.

3.9 Arranging and structuring a song

Arranging and structuring, for the purposes of this book, will refer to the following; The arrangement is the choice of instrumentation you decide to use. This could mean which synth bass patch you choose, whether or not you choose a real bass or a synth bass, or even how the bass part weaves in and out of the song. Perhaps the bass part is absent for the first half of a verse, but then comes in for the second half. Another example would be if you have a specific melody and you don't know if it should be played on a guitar or synthesizer. Those are all (to me) arrangement decisions. Structure, on the other hand, is the sequence that your song "sections" appear in, such as intro, verse, chorus, etc. Saying your song has an eight bar intro followed by verse, chorus, and second verse is describing your song's structure.

These terms may mean something slightly different (depending on who you ask), so I thought it would be wise to describe how I am using them in this book. Nonetheless how you arrange the different song parts in your composition, and what timbres you choose can make or break your track. When I was younger I used to overlook the importance of arrangement, and now I look back on that and laugh. The arrangement and structure of a song can have a big impact on the overall feel and emotion of the track, and it can make the difference between a good song and a great one.

Look at it like this; You're going to create a song with a bunch of parts. There's going to be a drum part, a bass part, probably some chords, perhaps a lead, and those are just the fundamental parts. If you design a song that features all of the parts layered together, with no changes… It's going to get boring very fast. Having all parts play together probably sounds extremely powerful, but if you don't keep things moving all you have is a nice loop… not a complete song. This is why when you listen to great music, it seems to always keep your interest. It doesn't get boring because it's always moving. This movement can be created in any number of ways. One rule of thumb you can use is to ask yourself, "how can I make this different, but not too different?" Examples might be using a different synth patch (or different instrument altogether) for the same melody in different parts of the song. Or, you could have two drum parts that are similar but slightly different and interchange them at will. Some arrangement choices can be extremely subtle, such as adding a minimal percussion track that is mixed into the background, or an equally subtle harmony part. Other times, the arrangement is much more overt with huge shifts in dynamics, instrumentation, and vibe.

Structure is important as well. It's important to not have an intro or a first verse that goes on too long. If you look at most top 40 hits, they almost always hit the first chorus within the first minute. This is not an accident. As the saying goes, "don't bore us, get to the chorus".

Synthwave music is influenced by the music of the 1980s, and as a result many of the song structures tend to resemble traditional pop-rock. Some longer, more progressive synthwave arrangements definitely exist, so don't be afraid to experiment! Song structures of synthwave music can vary widely, but some common structures include:

1. Intro - Verse - Chorus - Bridge - Verse - Chorus - Outro: This is a common structure that is often used in synthwave music. The intro sets the tone for the song and can include a synth melody or a drum pattern. The verse and chorus sections are where the main melody and lyrics are presented, and the bridge section can be used to introduce a different melody or change in rhythm. The outro can be used to bring the song to a close.

2. Verse - Chorus - Verse - Chorus - Breakdown - Outro: This is another common structure that is often used in synthwave music. The verse and chorus sections are where the main melody and lyrics are presented, and the breakdown section can be used to introduce a different melody or change in rhythm. The outro can be used to bring the song to a close.

3. Intro - Verse - Chorus - Verse - Chorus - Outro: A simpler structure that can be used for shorter tracks and focused on the core elements of the song.

4. Intro - Verse - Chorus - Verse - Chorus - Bridge - Verse - Chorus - Outro: This structure is similar to the first one but with an additional verse and chorus section, so the song can have more development and a longer running time.

5. Intro - Verse - Chorus - Breakdown - Outro: This structure is ideal for short tracks and focused on the core elements of the song, but with a breakdown section that can be used to introduce a different melody or change in rhythm

6. Instrumental: This structure is common in synthwave music, where the song is purely instrumental, with no vocals. This allows the musicians to focus on creating a retro-futuristic soundscape, where melody and rhythm are the main elements.

These are just a few examples of the common structures in synthwave music, and many other variations exist. The key is to keep in mind that the music should be focused on the melody, rhythm and harmony. And also to remember that the structure is not set in stone and can be modified to fit the song's needs.

Here are some more tips for arranging and structuring a song for synthwave music:

1. Start with a verse-chorus structure: The verse-chorus structure is a common arrangement technique used in synthwave music. This structure consists of a verse, which sets the scene and introduces the main theme of the song, followed by a chorus, which is the main hook or catchy part of the song.

2. Use a bridge or pre-chorus: A bridge or pre-chorus is a section of a song that comes before the chorus and provides a transition between the verse and the chorus. It can be used to build tension and create a sense of anticipation before the chorus.

3. Experiment with different section lengths: The length of the sections in a song can have a big impact on the overall feel and emotion of the track. Experiment with different section lengths to find the right balance for your song.

4. Use repetition: Repetition is a powerful tool in music arrangement. Repeating a melody, chord progression, or section of a song can create a sense of familiarity and make the song more memorable.

5. Use dynamics: Dynamics refer to the loudness or softness of a sound. Experiment with different dynamics to add depth and interest to your song. For example, starting a song with a soft and delicate melody and gradually building it up to a climax can create a sense of tension and release.

6. Add effects: Effects such as reverb, delay, and distortion can add character and texture to your song. Experiment with different effects to find the right balance for your song.

7. Experiment with different structures: There is no one-size-fits-all structure for synthwave music, so don't be afraid to experiment with different structures. For example, you can use an intro, verse, pre-chorus, chorus, verse, pre-chorus, chorus, and outro, or you can use an intro, verse, chorus, verse, chorus, middle 8, verse, chorus, and outro.

3.10 How to build a 3rd harmony

Remember intervals? Building a third interval harmony from any given scale is a technique that can add depth and complexity to your music. This technique involves transposing a lead part to the third interval of a scale, creating a harmony that complements the original melody. In this article, we will go over the steps of how to build a third interval harmony from any given scale.

Step 2: Identify the third interval
Assuming you know the scale of the lead part you're building a harmony from, the next step is to identify the third interval of each note in the lead part. In the case of the C major scale, the third interval is E. To find the third interval in any scale, you can count up three scale degrees from the root note.

Step 3: Transpose the lead part
Now that you have identified the third interval, the next step is to transpose the lead part to that interval. This can be done by simply moving the lead part up three semitones. In the case of the C major scale, you would transpose the lead part from C to E.

Step 4: Create the harmony
With the lead part transposed to the third interval, the next step is to create the harmony. This can be done by playing the transposed lead part along with the original lead part. In the case of the C major scale, you would play the C and E notes together, creating a harmony.

Step 5: Experiment with different chords
One way to create a more complex harmony is to experiment with different chords. You can do this by adding additional notes to the harmony, such as the fifth or seventh scale degree. For example, in the case of the C major scale, you can add G to the harmony of C and E, creating a C major chord.

Step 6: Experiment with different inversions
Another way to create a more complex harmony is to experiment with different inversions. An inversion is a way of rearranging the notes of a chord to create a different harmonic effect. For example, you can create an inversion of the C major chord by playing the E note as the lowest note, instead of the C note

.

Building a third interval harmony can add depth and complexity to your music. It's a technique that can be applied to any scale and can be used to create a wide range of harmonic possibilities. It's important to experiment with different chords and inversions, to find the combination that works best for your music. Remember that building a third interval harmony is not a set rule, it's a technique that you can use as a tool to make your composition more interesting and engaging.

Part IV: Sound Design

4.1 Techniques for creating and shaping synth sounds

In music, an instrument's unique sound is also called its timbre. Such as a guitar, a flute, and a sawtooth synth can all play middle C at 261 Hz, but they will all sound different because the timbre is different. Timbre is (for our purposes) interchangeable with the term "synth sound", or perhaps more accurately synth patch or synth preset.

As you can guess, a timbre is made unique by its specific combination of attack, sustain, decay, release, as well as other oscillations and modulations to the waveform- just like a synthesizer! It's no mistake that a synth's settings are the very factors that define timbre- with a synthesizer, you are *making* new sounds.

Sound design is a crucial aspect of producing synthwave music, as the genre heavily relies on the use of synthetic sounds. Sound design techniques involve creating and shaping sounds using synthesizers, effects, and other tools. Here are some tips for creating and shaping synth sounds in synthwave music:

1. Start with a waveform: Synthesizers generate sound by oscillating or vibrating at a certain frequency. The waveform of a sound refers to the shape of the oscillation, and it can have a big impact on the overall character of the sound. Common waveforms used in synthwave music include sawtooth, square, and triangle.

2. Use filters: Filters are used to shape the tone of a sound by cutting or boosting certain frequencies. Common types of filters used in synthwave music include low-pass, high-pass, and band-pass filters. Low-pass filters are used to remove high frequencies, high-pass filters are used to remove low frequencies, and band-pass filters are used to isolate a specific range of frequencies.

3. Experiment with envelopes: Envelopes are used to shape the attack, decay, sustain, and release of a sound. Experimenting with different envelope settings can add depth and interest to your synth sounds.

4. Use modulation: Modulation is the process of using one signal to control another. Common types of modulation used in synthwave music include frequency modulation (FM) and amplitude modulation (AM). FM is used to create complex harmonic structures, while AM is used to create tremolo or vibrato effects.

5. Use effects: Effects such as reverb, delay, and distortion can add character and texture to your synth sounds. Experiment with different effects to find the right balance for your track.

6. Use software synthesizers: Software synthesizers are a powerful tool for sound design, as they offer a wide range of features and capabilities. Popular software synthesizers for synthwave music production include Serum, Omnisphere, and Massive.

7. Sample and resample: Sampling is the process of recording and reusing a sound or a phrase. You can sample your own sounds or use samples from other sources. Resampling is the process of recording a sound or a phrase and using it as a source for further sound design.

8. Layer sounds: Layering different sounds can add depth and complexity to your synth sounds. Try layering different waveforms, filters, or effects to create unique and interesting sounds.

Sound design is a crucial aspect of producing synthwave music. Experimenting with different waveforms, filters, envelopes, modulation, effects, software synthesizers, sampling, and layering techniques can make a huge difference in the way an arrangement is perceived.

4.2 Examples of synthwave sounds

1. Bass: "Sub Bass" is a popular synthwave timbre that can be heard in many songs in the genre. It is a deep, warm, and slightly distorted bass sound that is typically created using a virtual or hardware synthesizer with a low-pass filter. It is often used to provide a solid foundation for the rest of the mix and can be heard in songs such as "Midnight City" by M83 and "A Real Hero" by College & Electric Youth. It is often associated with the Roland SH-101 or Moog Minitaur.

2. Lead: "Lead synth" is a popular synthwave timbre that is often used to create melodic hooks and catchy riffs in the genre. It is typically created using a virtual or hardware synthesizer with a sawtooth waveform and a high-pass filter. It is often used to create a bright, cutting, and melodic sound that stands out in the mix and can be heard in songs such as "Nightcall" by Kavinsky and "The Grid" by Daft Punk. It is often associated with Roland Jupiter-8 or Moog Memorymoog

3. Pad: "Pad synth" is a popular synthwave timbre that is often used to provide a sense of atmosphere and depth in the genre. It is typically created using a virtual or hardware synthesizer with a slow attack, long release, and a low-pass filter. It is often used to create a warm, lush, and spacious sound that fills out the mix and can be heard in songs such as "Early Summer" by The Midnight and "Echoes" by Lazerhawk. It is often associated with Roland D-50 or Yamaha DX7

4. Arpeggio: "Arpeggio synth" is a popular synthwave timbre that is often used to create complex and evolving patterns in the genre. It is typically created using a virtual or hardware synthesizer with a step sequencer, arpeggiator, or a combination of both. It is

often used to create a repetitive, hypnotic, and driving sound that is layered over the rest of the mix and can be heard in songs such as "Fury" by Timecop1983 and "Fading" by Mitch Murder. It is often associated with Roland SH-101 or Moog Minitaur

5. Pluck: "Pluck synth" is a popular synthwave timbre that is often used to create sharp and syncopated synth lines that complement the bass and drums. It is typically created using a virtual or hardware synthesizer with a square waveform and a low-pass filter. It is often used to create a sharp and cutting sound that stands out in the mix and can be heard in songs such as "Voyager" by The Midnight and "Echoes" by Lazerhawk. It is often associated with Roland SH-101 or Moog Minitaur

6. Chord: "Chord synth" is a popular synthwave timbre that is often used to create complex chord progressions and harmonies in the genre. It is typically created using a virtual or hardware synthesizer with a chord mode or a combination of multiple synths. It is often used to create a rich and harmonic sound that fills out the mix and can be heard in songs such as "Midnight City" by M83 and "A Real Hero" by College & Electric Youth. It is often associated with Roland Jupiter-8 or Moog Memorymoog

7. Celeste: "Celeste synth" is a popular synthwave timbre that is often used to create a bright and shimmering bell-like sound. It is typically created using a virtual or hardware synthesizer with a sine waveform and a high-pass filter. It is often used to create a sense of wonder and nostalgia in the mix and can be heard in songs such as "The Night" by The Midnight and "Echoes" by Lazerhawk. It is often associated with Roland D-50 or Yamaha DX7.

8. Bell: "Bell synth" is a popular synthwave timbre that is often used to create a bright and metallic bell-like sound. It is typically created using a virtual or hardware synthesizer with a sawtooth waveform and a high-pass filter. It is often used to create a sense of wonder and nostalgia in the mix and can be heard in songs such as "The Night" by The Midnight and "Echoes" by Lazerhawk. It is often associated with Roland D-50 or Yamaha DX7.

9. Poly: "Poly synth" is a popular synthwave timbre that is often used to create rich and complex chordal sounds. It is typically created using a virtual or hardware synthesizer with multiple oscillators, filters, and modulation options. It is often used to create a sense of depth and complexity in the mix and can be heard in songs such as "Midnight City" by M83 and "A Real Hero" by College & Electric Youth. It is often associated with the Roland Jupiter-8 (and the Jupiter-8's many clones) or the Moog Memorymoog

10. Sync: "Sync synth" is a popular synthwave timbre that is often used to create fast and syncopated synth lines. It is typically created using a virtual or hardware synthesizer with a sawtooth waveform and a sync option, allowing the oscillators to lock in phase. It is often used to create a sense of energy and movement in the mix and can be heard in songs such as "Fury" by Timecop1983 and "Fading" by Mitch Murder. It is often associated with Roland SH-101 or Moog Minitaur.

11. Sitar: "Sitar synth" is a popular synthwave timbre that is often used to create a sitar-like sound. It is typically created using a virtual or hardware synthesizer with a complex waveform and a high-pass filter. It is often used to create a sense of mystery and exoticism in the mix and can be heard in songs such as "Echoes" by Lazerhawk and "The Grid" by Daft Punk. It is often associated with Roland D-50 or Yamaha DX7.

12. Flute: "Flute synth" is a popular synthwave timbre that is often used to create a flute-like sound. It is typically created using a virtual or hardware synthesizer with a sine waveform and a high-pass filter. It is often used to create a sense of wonder and nostalgia in the mix and can be heard in songs such as "The Night" by The Midnight and "Echoes" by Lazerhawk.

General approaches towards leads

1. Analog-style leads: Analog-style leads are a staple of synthwave music, and are often used to create a retro, nostalgic feel. These leads are characterized by a warm, rich sound that evokes the sound of vintage analog synthesizers. Examples of this sound can be heard in tracks by popular synthwave artists like Com Truise and The Midnight.
2. FM leads: FM leads are another popular choice in synthwave music, characterized by a bright, sharp sound that is often used to create a sense of tension and drama. These leads are often associated with the Yamaha DX7 synthesizer, and can be heard in tracks by popular synthwave artists like Lazerhawk and Mitch Murder.
3. PWM leads: Pulse-width modulation leads are a unique and distinctive sound in synthwave music, characterized by a complex, modulated sound that is often used to create a sense of movement and energy. These leads are often associated with the Roland Jupiter-8 synthesizer, and can be heard in tracks by popular synthwave artists like The Outrunners and Futurecop!
4. Supersaw leads: Supersaw leads are a popular choice in synthwave music, characterized by a complex, rich sound that is often used to create a sense of motion and energy. These leads are often associated with the Roland JP-8000 synthesizer, and can be heard in tracks by popular synthwave artists like Lazerhawk and Mitch Murder.
5. Phase leads: Phase leads are another popular choice in synthwave music, characterized by a bright, sharp sound that is often used to create a sense of tension and drama. These leads are often associated with the Roland SH-101 synthesizer, and can be heard in tracks by popular synthwave artists like The Midnight and Kavinsky.
6. Guitar leads: Guitar leads are also commonly used in synthwave music, often with a clean tone, with echo and delay effects, to create a retro and nostalgic feel. These leads are often associated with the Fender Stratocaster and can be heard in tracks by popular synthwave artists like Mitch Murder and The Midnight.

Some general rules of timbre to fall back on

1. Start with a bass sound you like, as this (along with your drum sounds) are going to be the basis for your track.

2. Don't be afraid to use presets. Modify them as needed, and learn to make your own sounds by studying the presets you like. Lots of professionals and famous producers use presets, so don't feel bad about it.

3. In general, you want to design your synth patches with different frequency ranges in mind. Obviously, not everything can be a fat bass sound, or a bright and sparkling high-freq sound, etc. Not everything can occupy the same space at the same time, and if you try it, sounds get masked, and the mix turns to mud. In order to avoid this, think of synth patches (and instrumentation/timbre in general) in terms of frequency ranges. Your bass patch should occupy the bass range, the pads and chord rhythms should fall into the low-mids to midrange, and lead parts should be in the upper midrange and above. Most of the "upper end" of the frequency range is mostly sweetening in the mix stage, as human hearing is mostly focused in the midrange frequencies.

4.3 Using samples and drum machines

Using samples and drum machines is an essential aspect of sound design when producing synthwave music. Samples are pre-recorded sounds that can be used to create new sounds and add character and texture to a track. Drum machines are electronic musical instruments that produce a variety of drum sounds. Here are some tips for using samples and drum machines in the sound design process when producing synthwave music:

1. Use drum samples: Drum samples are pre-recorded drum sounds that can be used to create beats and add a retro feel to a track. There are a variety of drum sample packs available, including samples of classic drum machines such as the Roland TR-808 and LinnDrum.

2. Use drum machines: Drum machines are electronic musical instruments that produce a variety of drum sounds. They are often used to create beats and add a retro feel to a track. Popular drum machines used in synthwave include Roland TR-808, LinnDrum, and Roland TR-909.

3. Experiment with different samples: Experimenting with different samples can help you to find the right sounds for your track. Try using samples from different sources, such as old records, vintage synthesizers, and classic drum machines.

4. Use sample chops: Sample chops are short snippets of samples that are edited and rearranged to create new sounds. Experiment with chopping and rearranging samples to create unique and interesting sounds.

5. Use sample layering: Layering different samples can add depth and complexity to a track. Try layering different samples, such as drums, percussion, and synths, to create a rich and textured sound.

6. Use sample stretching: Sample stretching is the process of changing the tempo of a sample without changing its pitch. Experimenting with sample stretching can create interesting and unique sounds.

7. Use MIDI drum patterns: MIDI drum patterns are sequences of MIDI notes that can be used to control a drum machine or a drum sample. Try using different MIDI drum patterns to add a retro feel to your track.

8. Use drum machine emulations: There are a variety of software drum machine emulations available, such as the Roland TR-808 and LinnDrum emulations. These software emulations can be used to create a retro feel in your tracks without the need for a physical drum machine.

Drum sounds

1. Gated snare: The gated snare is a signature sound of synthwave music, characterized by a sharp, short snare sound that is often used in combination with a reverb effect to create a dramatic, explosive sound. This sound is often associated with the Roland TR-808 drum machine, and can be heard in tracks by popular synthwave artists like Com Truise and Miami Nights 1984.

2. 808 cowbell: The cowbell sound from the Roland TR-808 drum machine is a popular choice in synthwave music, often used to add a sense of rhythmic drive and energy to a track. This sound can be heard in songs by artists like Kavinsky and The Midnight.

3. Claps: Claps are a staple of synthwave music, and are often used to accentuate the beat and add a sense of energy to a track. This sound is often associated with the Roland TR-808 drum machine, and can be heard in tracks by popular synthwave artists like Lazerhawk and Mitch Murder.

4. Laser-tom: Laser-toms are a unique and distinctive sound in synthwave music, characterized by a sharp, high-pitched sound that evokes the image of laser beams. This sound is often associated with the Roland TR-808 drum machine, and can be heard in tracks by popular synthwave artists like The Outrunners and Futurecop!

5. Snare rolls: Snare rolls are a popular choice in synthwave music, characterized by a fast, repeating snare sound that creates a sense of motion and energy. This sound is

often associated with the Roland TR-808 drum machine and can be heard in tracks by popular synthwave artists like Lazerhawk and Mitch Murder.

6. Hi-hat: Hi-hat is a staple of synthwave music, and is often used to add a sense of rhythmic drive and energy to a track. This sound is often associated with the Roland TR-808 drum machine, and can be heard in tracks by popular synthwave artists like The Midnight and Lazerhawk.

Using samples and drum machines is an essential aspect of sound design when producing synthwave music. Experimenting with different samples, sample chops, sample layering, sample stretching, MIDI drum patterns, and drum machine emulations can help you to create unique and interesting sounds that add character and texture to your tracks. With the right samples and drum machine, you can create a retro feel that is typical of synthwave music.

4.4 Bass synth sound design

1. Analog-style: This approach towards synthwave bass lines is heavily influenced by the bass sounds and patterns of analog synthesizers from the 1980s. The basslines are often created using virtual analog synthesizers or hardware synths, such as the Roland SH-101 or Moog Minitaur, and have a distinct warm, rich, and round tone. Examples of common synthwave bass parts in this style include the use of syncopated 16th-note patterns, arpeggiated sequences, and syncopated octave jumps. Examples of songs that use this style include "Nightcall" by Kavinsky and "The Grid" by Daft Punk.

2. Sequenced: This approach towards synthwave bass lines is heavily influenced by the use of sequencers in electronic music production. The basslines often have a repetitive and hypnotic feel, with a focus on precise and steady 16th-note patterns, and use of step-sequencing to create complex and evolving basslines. Examples of common synthwave bass parts in this style include the use of syncopated 16th-note patterns, arpeggiated sequences, and syncopated octave jumps. Examples of songs that use this style include "Early Summer" by The Midnight and "Echoes" by Lazerhawk.

3. Subtractive: This approach towards synthwave bass lines is heavily influenced by the use of subtractive synthesis in electronic music production. The basslines often have a more aggressive and distorted feel, with a focus on precise and steady 16th-note patterns, and use of subtractive synthesis to create complex and evolving basslines. Examples of common synthwave bass parts in this style include the use of syncopated 16th-note patterns, arpeggiated sequences, and syncopated octave jumps. Examples of songs that use this style include "Fury" by Timecop1983 and "Fading" by Mitch Murder.

4. Fusion: This approach towards synthwave bass lines is heavily influenced by the fusion of different genres. The basslines often have a more fusion of the 80s retro and the present, with a focus on precise and steady 16th-note patterns, and use of various synthesis techniques to create complex and evolving basslines. Examples of common synthwave bass parts in this style include the use of syncopated 16th-note patterns, arpeggiated sequences, and syncopated octave jumps. Examples of songs that use this style include "Voyager" by The Midnight and "Echoes" by Lazerhawk.

4.5 Adding effects such as reverb and delay

Adding effects such as reverb and delay is an important aspect of sound design when producing synthwave music. Effects can add character, texture, and depth to a track, and they can be used to create a sense of space and atmosphere. Here are some tips for using reverb and delay effects when producing synthwave music:

1. Use reverb: Reverb is an effect that simulates the sound of a sound reflecting off of surfaces in a room or space. It can be used to add depth and dimension to a track. Try using different reverb settings, such as room, hall, and plate, to find the right sound for your track.

2. Use delay: Delay is an effect that creates a repetition of a sound. It can be used to add depth, texture, and interest to a track. Try using different delay settings, such as quarter-note delay, dotted-eighth delay, and ping-pong delay, to find the right sound for your track.

3. Experiment with different reverb and delay settings: Experimenting with different reverb and delay settings can help you to find the right sound for your track. Try adjusting the decay time, wet/dry mix, and feedback to create unique and interesting sounds.

4. Use stereo imaging: Stereo imaging is the process of creating a sense of width and space in a track. Try using stereo reverb and delay effects to create a sense of space and atmosphere in your track.

5. Use modulation effects: Modulation effects such as chorus and flanger can be used to add movement and interest to a track. Try using modulation effects in conjunction with reverb and delay to create unique and interesting sounds.

6. Use parallel processing: Parallel processing is the process of routing a sound through multiple effects at the same time. Try using parallel processing to add depth and texture to your reverb and delay effects.

7. Use software effects: Software effects such as plugins are a powerful tool for sound design. There are a variety of reverb and delay plugins available, such as ValhallaRoom, and Eventide's Stereo Room. These plugins can provide a wide range of reverb and delay effects that can be used to shape the sound of your track.

Adding effects such as reverb and delay is an important aspect of sound design when producing synthwave music. Experimenting with different reverb and delay settings, stereo imaging, modulation effects, parallel processing, and software effects can help you to create unique and interesting sounds that add character and texture to your tracks. The use of these effects can add depth and width to the sound and also create a retro feel that is typical of synthwave music.

4.6 Analog Synth Controls

Analog synthesizers are a popular choice among synthwave musicians, as they offer a wide range of sound-shaping options and a unique, warm sound. Here are some basic audio synthesis controls, functions, and techniques that you might use with an analog synthesizer:

1. Oscillators: An oscillator is a sound-generating component of a synthesizer that produces a basic waveform, such as a sine, square, or sawtooth wave. Most analog synthesizers have multiple oscillators that can be used to create complex sounds by layering and modulating different waveforms.
2. VCO (Voltage-Controlled Oscillator): A VCO is a type of oscillator that generates sound by controlling the voltage applied to it. This allows for precise control over the pitch of the oscillator, and can be modulated using other synthesizer components such as LFOs or envelopes.
3. LFO (Low-Frequency Oscillator): An LFO is a type of oscillator that generates a waveform at a low frequency, typically below 20Hz. This waveform can be used to modulate other synthesizer components, such as the pitch or amplitude of an oscillator, to create effects such as vibrato or tremolo.
4. Attack, Decay, Sustain, Release (ADSR): These are four parameters that control the amplitude envelope of a sound. Attack is the time it takes for the sound to reach its maximum amplitude, decay is the time it takes for the sound to decrease to the sustain level, sustain is the level at which the sound is held, and release is the time it takes for the sound to decrease to silence after the key is released.
5. Filters: A filter is a component that is used to shape the sound by cutting or boosting certain frequencies. Low-pass filters allow lower frequencies to pass through and cut higher frequencies, while high-pass filters allow higher frequencies

4.7 Digital vs. Analog

The debate between analog and digital synthesizers is a long-standing one in the music production community. Analog synthesizers use analog circuits to generate sound, while digital synthesizers use digital signal processing (DSP) to create sound. Both have their own unique set of advantages and disadvantages.

Analog Synthesizers Pros:
- They have a warm, organic sound that is often considered to be more natural and pleasing to the ear.
- They have a tactile, hands-on interface that allows for more improvisation and experimentation in sound design.
- They are often considered to be more reliable and durable than digital synthesizers.
- They have a limited number of parameters, which can make them more intuitive to use.

Analog Synthesizers Cons:
- They are typically more expensive than digital synthesizers.
- They can be less precise and accurate than digital synthesizers.
- They have a limited number of parameters, which can make it harder to create complex sounds.
- They are more sensitive to temperature and humidity changes.

Digital Synthesizers Pros:
- They have a wide range of sound-shaping options and can create complex and detailed sounds, with more modern sound-design features.
- They are often more affordable than analog synthesizers.
- They are more precise and accurate than analog synthesizers.
- They can emulate the sound of other instruments and sound sources. Digital synths like ROMplers provide a huge sound palette in a single instrument.

Digital Synthesizers Cons:
- Some say they can have a sterile or artificial sound that is often considered less pleasing than the warm, organic sound of analog synthesizers. I tend to disagree, but it is a popular opinion.
- They can be less intuitive to use, with a more complex interface.
- They can be more prone to malfunction or failure than analog synthesizers.
- Set-up, which may involve a computer, can be a hassle for some.
- Similarly, software synths that require a computer can suffer from latency issues, especially during live performances.

Both analog and digital synthesizers have their own unique set of advantages and disadvantages. Whether to choose one or the other depends on the individual's preferences, needs and budget. Analog synthesizers offer a warm and organic sound, a hands-on interface that can be played musically, and a more intuitive layout. On the other hand, digital synthesizers offer a wide range of modern sound-shaping options, more convenience, a smaller form factor, overall higher fidelity, and a more affordable price point. In the end, the choice is yours.

Part V: Tracking

5.1 Recording MIDI vs. audio

Tracking audio and tracking MIDI are two different methods of recording music in a home studio.
Tracking audio refers to the process of recording audio signals directly into a computer or other digital audio workstation (DAW) using a microphone or other audio input device. This can include recording vocals, live instruments such as guitar or drums, or external sound sources such as a synthesizer or drum machine. Audio recording allows you to capture a performance exactly as it is played, including any nuances or imperfections in the performance.

On the other hand, tracking MIDI refers to the process of recording MIDI data into a computer or DAW. MIDI, or Musical Instrument Digital Interface, is a protocol that allows electronic musical instruments and computers to communicate with each other. MIDI data contains information such as note on/off messages, velocity, and controller data, but no audio. This data can be used to control software instruments or external sound modules, allowing for precise editing and manipulation of the performance.

Tracking audio is the process of recording audio signals directly into a computer or DAW, capturing the nuances and imperfections of a performance, while tracking MIDI is the process of recording MIDI data, which is a set of instructions that can be used to control software instruments or external sound modules, allowing for precise editing and manipulation of the performance.

5.2 MIDI - step recording vs. real-time recording.

When recording MIDI in a DAW, step-recording refers to the process of inputting MIDI notes into the DAW one at a time, usually by clicking and dragging with a mouse. This can be a very precise method of inputting MIDI, but can also be time-consuming and tedious.

On the other hand, recording MIDI in real-time using a piano-key style MIDI controller allows the musician to play the notes in a more natural and fluid manner, similar to playing a piano. This can be a more efficient method of inputting MIDI, as the musician is able to play the part they want to record without the need for stopping and starting. Additionally, this method can be useful for capturing the nuances and expressiveness of the performance.

Examples of piano-key style MIDI controllers include the Akai MPK Mini and the M-Audio Keystation. These controllers typically have a range of piano-style keys and often include additional buttons, knobs, and sliders for controlling various aspects of the performance and recording.

It's worth mentioning that some DAWs like Ableton Live have features like "Arrangement View" where you can record MIDI clips in real-time and then edit them afterwards, which can provide the best of both worlds.

5.3 MIDI quantization

No book on recording MIDI would be complete without an explanation and use-cases for quantization. MIDI quantization is the process of automatically adjusting the timing of MIDI notes so that they align to a specific rhythmic grid. This helps to tighten up the timing and make the MIDI performance more consistent and in time with the beat. Essentially, this corrects bad or inconsistent rhythm playing.

Quantization is often derided for being "cheating", or sounding "robotic", and perhaps those things are true on some level. However, there is no doubt that the in-human and machine-like rhythm of a sequencer, along with aggressive quantization is what creates "the sound" of modern electronic music. Everything to come from the musical tree of 1980s "techno", and including new-wave music of the time used the robotic sound of rhythm machines as a feature of the style.

One example of using quantization while recording a MIDI part for a song is adjusting the timing of a piano part so that all the notes are perfectly in time with the beat of the drum track. Another example is quantizing the timing of a bassline to make it groove better with the drum track. By quantizing MIDI notes, you can clean up the performance and make the timing more precise, which can greatly improve the overall sound of the recording.

In Reaper, you can utilize quantization while in the MIDI editor by pressing the "Q" button in the top control panel as shown in image 5.3A

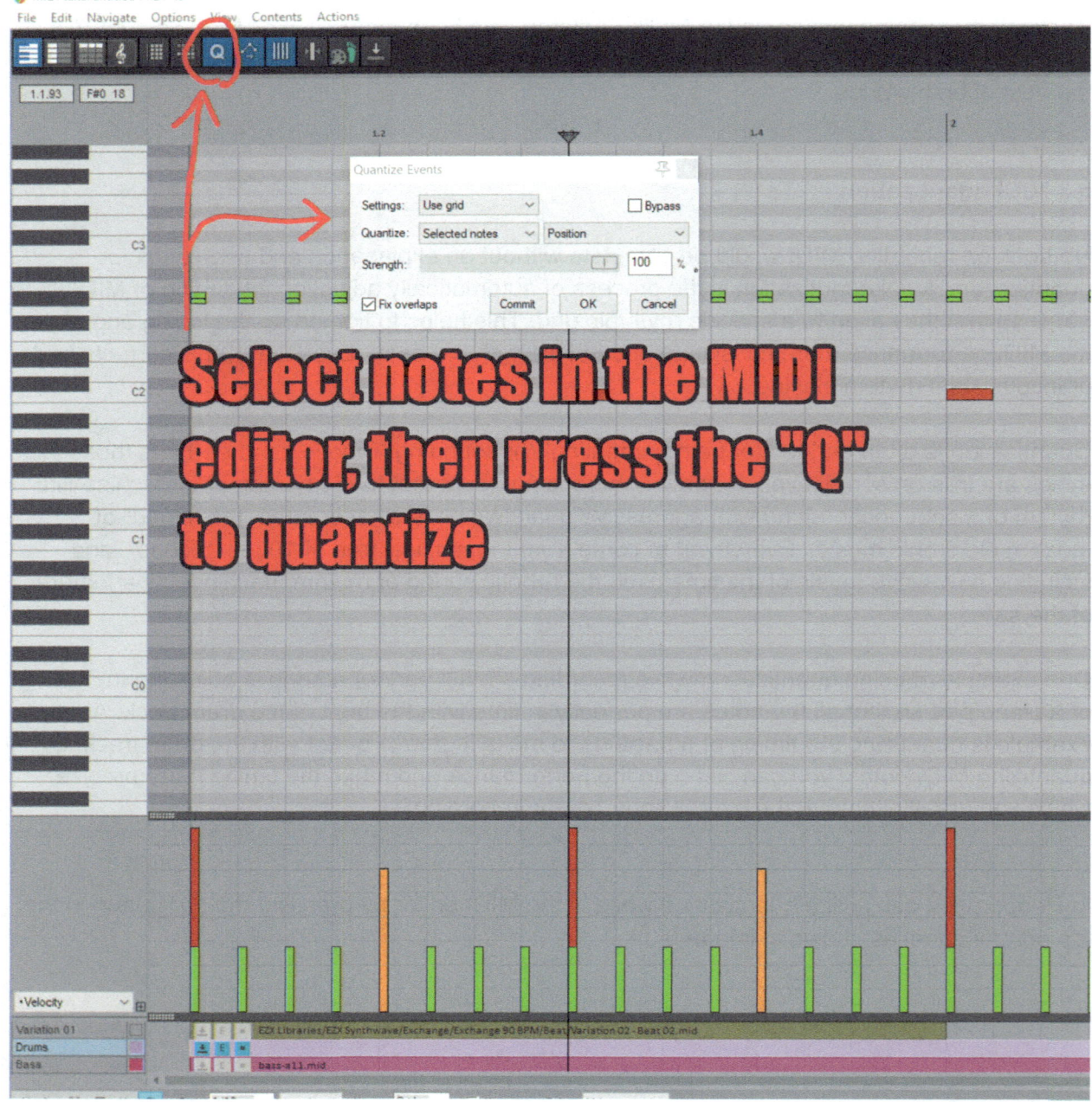

Image 5.3A

5.3 Recording a drum beat

Tracking MIDI drums in a home studio involves a few steps, but it can be done fairly easily with the right equipment and software. Here is a simple yet complete explanation on how to track MIDI drums:

1. Connect your MIDI controller to your computer: To track MIDI drums, you will need a MIDI controller, such as an electronic drum kit or a MIDI keyboard, that is connected to your computer via USB or MIDI cables.
2. Load a drum instrument in your DAW: Next, you will need to load a drum instrument in your DAW (Digital Audio Workstation) software. This can be a software instrument such as a virtual drum machine or a sample library, or an external sound module connected to your computer via MIDI.
3. Set up your MIDI controller: You will then need to set up your MIDI controller in your DAW, by creating a new MIDI track and assigning it to the drum instrument you loaded in step 2. This will allow you to control the instrument with your MIDI controller.
4. Begin recording: Once your MIDI controller and drum instrument are set up, you can begin recording. You can either record in real-time by playing the MIDI controller or step record by inputting the MIDI notes one at a time.

Composing a simple 4/4 drum beat with the kick on 1, and the snare on 3 is a fundamental skill for any music producer. This type of beat is known as the "four-on-the-floor" beat and it's commonly used in various genres of music including synthwave, techno, and house. In this article, we'll go over the steps of how to compose a 4/4 drum beat with the kick on 1, and the snare on 3.

Step 1: Choose a tempo
The first step in composing a 4/4 drum beat is to choose a tempo. The tempo is the speed of the beat, measured in beats per minute (BPM). For a simple 4/4 drum beat, a tempo of around 120 BPM is a good starting point. However, you can experiment with different tempos to find what works best for your music.

Step 2: Place the kick on 1
With the tempo set, the next step is to place the kick drum on the first beat of the bar. In 4/4 time, this is the first beat of the measure. You can use a software or hardware drum machine, or a drum sample library to create your kick drum sound.

Step 3: Place the snare on 3
With the kick drum in place, the next step is to place the snare drum on the third beat of the bar. In 4/4 time, this is the third beat of the measure. You can use a software or hardware drum machine, or a drum sample library to create your snare drum sound.

Step 4: Add hi-hats
With the kick and snare in place, the next step is to add hi-hats. Hi-hats can be used to add more texture and rhythm to the beat. A common pattern for the hi-hats is to play 8th notes, which means that the hi-hats will play twice for each beat of the measure. This will give the beat a sense of movement and flow.

Step 5: Experiment with variations

With the basic 4/4 drum beat in place, the next step is to experiment with variations. This could include adding additional drum sounds, such as a clap or a tambourine, or changing the rhythm of the kick or snare. You could also try changing the tempo, or experimenting with different time signatures. The possibilities are endless, so feel free to get creative and experiment with different sounds and rhythms. You may want to record these on a different track, especially if using completely different sounds like percussion, claps, or additional sounds. That way you preserve the integrity of your main drum part, and it allows you to mix them later.

Composing a 4/4 drum beat with the kick on 1, and the snare on 3 is a fundamental skill for any music producer. It's a simple but effective pattern that can be used in various genres of music. By following these steps, you can create your own 4/4 drum beat, but don't be afraid to experiment with different variations and add effects to make it unique. Remember that the possibilities are endless and the most important thing is to have fun and enjoy the process.

Tracking MIDI drums involves connecting a MIDI controller to a computer, loading a drum instrument in a DAW, setting up the MIDI controller, recording the drum track, editing and refining the track, and finally mixing and exporting the track.

5.4 Recording a bass line

Tracking a MIDI bass line in a home studio involves a few steps, but it can be done fairly easily with the right equipment and software. Here is a simple yet complete explanation on how to track a MIDI bass line:

1. Connect your MIDI controller to your computer: To track a MIDI bass line, you will need a MIDI controller, such as a MIDI keyboard or a pad controller, that is connected to your computer via USB or MIDI cables.

2. Load a bass instrument in your DAW: Next, you will need to load a bass instrument in your DAW (Digital Audio Workstation) software. This can be a software instrument such as a virtual bass or a sample library, or an external sound module connected to your computer via MIDI.

3. Set up your MIDI controller: You will then need to set up your MIDI controller in your DAW, by creating a new MIDI track and assigning it to the bass instrument you loaded in step 2. This will allow you to control the instrument with your MIDI controller.

4. Begin recording: Once your MIDI controller and bass instrument are set up, you can begin recording. You can either record in real-time by playing the MIDI controller or step record by inputting the MIDI notes one at a time.

5. Edit and refine your bass line: Once you have recorded your bass line, you can edit and refine it using the editing tools in your DAW. This can include adjusting the velocity, quantizing the timing, or adding effects such as reverb or distortion.

6. Mix and export your bass line: Finally, you can mix your bass line with the other tracks in your song and export it as an audio file or a MIDI file.

Tracking a MIDI bass line involves connecting a MIDI controller to a computer, loading a bass instrument in a DAW, setting up the MIDI controller, recording the bass line, editing and refining the track, and finally mixing and exporting the track.

5.5 Recording pads, leads, and other synthesizers

Recording leads, pads, and other synthesizer parts are, from an engineering standpoint, not very different from recording other synthesizer song parts.

5.6 Recording guitars

Recording electric guitars in a home studio can be done in a few different ways, but here is a simple yet complete explanation on how to record electric guitars using an audio interface:

1. Connect your guitar to your audio interface: To record electric guitars, you will need to connect your guitar to an audio interface using a standard 1/4" instrument cable. The audio interface will convert the analog signal from your guitar into a digital signal that can be recorded into your computer.

2. Set up your audio interface: Once your guitar is connected to the audio interface, you will need to set up the audio interface in your DAW (Digital Audio Workstation) software. This typically involves selecting the audio interface as the input source in your DAW's settings.

3. Choose a microphone and place it in front of the amplifier: To record the sound of your electric guitar, you will need to use a microphone placed in front of the amplifier. This can be either a dynamic or a condenser microphone. It's important to place the microphone in the right position to capture the desired tone, usually pointing the mic to the center of the speaker.

4. Set the levels and begin recording: Once your audio interface and microphone are set up, you can set the levels and begin recording. You will need to adjust the levels so that the audio is not clipping (too loud) or too quiet. It's recommended to use headphones for monitoring the recording.

5. Edit and refine your guitar track: Once you have recorded your guitar track, you can edit and refine it using the editing tools in your DAW. This can include adjusting the volume, panning, and adding effects such as reverb or distortion.

6. Mix and export your guitar track: Finally, you can mix your guitar track with the other tracks in your song and export it as an audio file.

Recording electric guitars in a home studio involves connecting the guitar to an audio interface, setting up the audio interface in the DAW, choosing a microphone and placing it in front of the amplifier, setting the levels, recording, editing and refining the track, and finally mixing and exporting the track.

5.7 Recording vocals

Recording vocals is an important aspect of music production, and it's essential to have a proper signal chain and environment to ensure that your recordings sound clear and professional. Here's an article on how to set up a proper signal chain and environment for recording vocals:

Step 1: Setting up the microphone
The first step in setting up a proper signal chain for recording vocals is to set up the microphone in a mic stand. Make sure the stand is sturdy and at the correct height for the vocalist. Position the microphone so that the diaphragm (the part of the microphone that converts sound into electrical signals) is at the same level as the vocalist's mouth. This will ensure that the microphone is capturing the sound at the right angle and distance.

Step 2: Proper mic placement
Proper mic placement is crucial for capturing a clear and natural sound. The best way to position the microphone is about 6 to 12 inches away from the vocalist's mouth. This distance will allow the microphone to capture the full range of the vocalist's voice without any proximity effect (a bass boost that occurs when the microphone is too close to the source). It's also important to note that the angle of the microphone should be pointed slightly upwards towards the vocalist's mouth to capture the sound correctly.

Step 3: Using a vocal shield
A vocal shield is a foam or fabric shield that is placed behind the microphone to reduce reflections and ambient noise. This will help to isolate the vocalist's voice and prevent unwanted sounds from being picked up by the microphone.

Step 4: Proper mic technique
Proper mic technique is essential for recording clear and professional vocals. The vocalist should be facing the microphone and keep the same distance from the mic throughout the

recording. The vocalist should also be mindful of their breathing and try to avoid breathing directly into the microphone. It's also important to avoid any excessive movement or handling of the microphone as this can cause unwanted noise in the recording.

Step 5: Monitor the recording

After setting up the microphone, it's important to monitor the recording to ensure that it's capturing the sound correctly. This can be done by listening to the sound through headphones or speakers. If the sound is unclear or muffled, make adjustments to the microphone position and technique until it sounds clear and professional.

Recording vocals is an important aspect of music production and it's essential to have a proper signal chain and environment to ensure that your recordings sound clear and professional. By following these steps, you can set up a microphone in a mic stand, proper mic placement, use of a vocal shield and proper mic technique, you can ensure that your vocals are recorded with the best quality. Remember that practice and experimentation are the keys to being a great vocalist.

Pop filter

Vocal shield

Condenser microphone

Shockmount for mic

Mic stands

XLR cable

Image 5.7A

This image shows a typical set-up for a vocal microphone, along with a vocal shield, pop-filter, shockmount, and mic stands.

Part VI: Mixing and Mastering

6.1 My basic theory on mixing

All in all, mixing isn't the dark art that some make it out to be. Simply, you're adjusting the volume of each individual track so that together, they create a "mix" that represents the song the way you feel it should sound. You will also add EQ and effects to each individual track (as necessary) in order to sonically sculpt that specific sound in a way that influences the whole as you see fit. Obviously, this is a highly personal (subjective) matter.

As I mentioned in our chapter on sound design, the goal is really to make sure that every instrument has its own place in the frequency spectrum. In other words, make sure that there aren't too many mix elements (i..e instruments, vocals, and other sounds) fighting each other in the same frequency range. This means that we'll be using EQ to alter the frequency profile of our separate tracks where necessary. As I was saying earlier, it helps immensely if your arrangement is planned out with this in mind. I.e. which instruments will carry your bass part, which will carry your midrange and high frequencies, etc.

Most times, while trying to make elements "fit" into a mix, **I will use subtractive EQ**. This means that instead of adding gain to accentuate certain frequencies, I will subtract what is not needed. This usually makes for a much cleaner mixing experience, and "creates space" for other elements rather than adding energy to your mix and potentially muddying things up. The exception is when trying to create a special effect, or if I just need to "hear more" of a certain frequency. In those instances, I will use additive EQ... but in 90% of mixing situations, while EQing an individual instrument or element, I will opt to subtract gain from a frequency range that isn't needed.

One of the major differences between mixing synthwave and other genres is the degree that you may have to heavily use EQ and other effects (like compression or reverb) to get the sound you're looking for. In other genres (like rock), mixing engineers take a much more "organic" approach to mixing synthesizers. I've seen many rock engineers suggest that synths and drum machines "don't need EQ", and there's some truth to this, but it really depends on the context. In synthwave this probably isn't the case, unless you're using sounds and samples with built-in or pre-recorded effects.

So without further adieu, here's my general theory on mixing. It's shockingly simple, and can apply to any musical genre— and it especially applies to synthwave, since it's even easier to apply to any sort of music that is mostly arranged and recorded with synthesizers. This theory is the "full spectrum" theory. Full spectrum theory states that with any piece of recorded music, you have a "full spectrum" of sonic frequencies to work with. This range of frequencies is the same for everyone (more or less), and is the same regardless of your musical genres, because this spectrum is also the range of human hearing, from 20Hz (20 Hertz), the lowest bass to 20kHz (20 kiloHertz), the highest high pitches. As I just stated, this is the range of human hearing, so we're talking about the highest and lowest pitches sounds that you, as a human being, can perceive with your ears. Your job while mixing is to fill this frequency range, from 20Hz to 20kHz, with a full arrangement of sounds. This means that you have to have different instruments (or song elements) playing in different sections within the spectrum, and these different musical parts should not overlap or occupy too much of the same "space". In other words, keep your bass part in the bass frequency range, etc. When you have more than one sound trying to occupy the same area in the frequency range, you get what is called "masking" where one of the sounds will seem to disappear behind the other sound that is appearing in the same range. This is because you can't distinctly hear two sounds with overlapping EQ profiles. The louder one always will be more apparent while the softer sound will blend into the louder one.

So, it's really that simple. You have a finite frequency spectrum, and you need to decide what sounds and instruments are going to occupy what general areas within that range. You don't need to be super specific, as these frequencies are not set in stone. This is an easier process with synthesizers for a few reasons. First, with synthesizers, you have a much more predictable frequency range that a given part will operate in. Secondly, due to the nature of MIDI and synthesis, it is a lot easier to change a given musical part to alter its frequency output so it better serves the mix. For instance, let's say I record a synth bass keyboard part in the wrong register. If I realize this while mixing, it's very easy to fix, as I can transpose the midi, or even change the octave output of the soft synthesizer itself. Conversely, let's say I record a bass guitar part as an audio file, and then realize it's in the wrong register. For an audio file, my only real recourse (without mangling the audio) would be to re-record with the same bassist, again.

So to recap the "Full spectrum" mixing method; Find out the frequency ranges of your various instrumental parts and/or tracks, and make sure they "fill" the entire spectrum. Make sure your arrangement is spaced out more or less evenly. Do not have multiple parts crowding the same part of the frequency spectrum, as they will blend into one tone and lose their distinction.

6.2 Instruments and their frequencies

Here's a chart listing common synthesizer sounds and their fundamental accompanying frequency ranges. Keep in mind that fundamental frequency doubles when going up an octave, and halves when going down an octave:

Synthesizer Sound	Frequency Range (Hz)
Distorted Electric Guitar	80-1000

Kick Drum	40-100
Snare Drum	200-600
808 Kick	40-100
Cowbell	500-1200
Clap	500-800
Bells	800-5000
Synth Arpeggio	500-8000
Laser Toms	300-1000
Hi-hat	3000-8000
Supersaw Lead	500-12000
Synth Pads	20-8000
Synth Bass	20-300
Reese Bass	20-300
Vocals	80-1000

Strings	80-1000
Choirs	80-1000

It's important to note that these are just general ranges and that the actual frequency range for a specific instrument/timbre can vary depending on various factors such as the type of synthesizer used, the sound design, and the recording/processing techniques applied. The fundamental frequency is also not the only important factor in determining the character and timbre of a sound, but it can give a good idea of the general range in which the sound lies in the frequency spectrum.

Also, keep in mind that you can use EQ and compression to "push" a single element into parts of the frequency range that it doesn't normally occupy. This is typically achieved by using parametric and shelving EQ boosts where necessary, and squishing tracks with compression to bring up the quiet over and undertones. This is actually a very useful (and often used) way of making a single instrument sound "huge" when soloed, or in a sparse mix. This is often the case when you want a single sound (like an arpeggio or pad) to appear big and wide during a breakdown.

6.3 Technique for Balancing and Equalizing Tracks

Balancing and equalizing tracks is an important aspect of mixing when producing synthwave music. The process of balancing and equalizing involves adjusting the levels and frequencies of the different elements in a track to create a cohesive and polished sound. Here are some tips for balancing and equalizing tracks when mixing synthwave music:

1. Use a reference track: Use a reference track to compare your mix to a professionally mixed and mastered track. This will help you to identify areas where your mix needs improvement and to make more accurate adjustments.

2. Balance the levels of the different elements: Make sure that the levels of the different elements in your mix are balanced. This will ensure that the different elements are heard clearly and that there are no elements that are overpowering others.

3. Use EQ to balance the frequencies: Use EQ to balance the frequencies of the different elements in your mix. This will ensure that the different elements are heard clearly and that there are no elements that are overpowering others.

4. Use a high-pass filter: Use a high-pass filter to remove unwanted low frequencies. This will help to clear up the low end of your mix and make room for the bass and kick drums.

5. Use a low-pass filter: Use a low-pass filter to remove unwanted high frequencies. This will help to clear up the high end of your mix and make room for the synths and percussion.

6. Use EQ to shape the sound of the different elements: Use EQ to shape the sound of the different elements in your mix. This will help to add character and interest to the different elements and to create a cohesive and polished sound.

7. Use compression: Compression can be used to control the dynamic range of a track and to add punch and power to the mix. Experiment with different compression settings to find the right balance for your track.

8. Use stereo imaging: Use stereo imaging techniques to create a sense of space and depth in your mix. Experiment with panning and stereo width to find the right balance for your track.

Balancing and equalizing tracks is an important aspect of mixing when producing synthwave music. The process of balancing and equalizing involves adjusting the levels and frequencies of the different elements in a track to create a cohesive and polished sound.

6.4 Reverb

Reverb is a common effect used in music production to add a sense of space and depth to a sound. When producing synthwave music, reverb can be used to create a sense of nostalgia and to add a retro feel to the music.

To use reverb while producing synthwave music, you would typically use a reverb plugin in your digital audio workstation (DAW) or an external hardware reverb processor. Reverb plugins and processors typically have several controls that can be adjusted to achieve the desired reverb sound:

1. Type: The type control sets the type of reverb algorithm used, such as hall, room, plate, or spring. Different types of reverbs are suited for different types of music, and each has its own unique characteristics.

2. Decay length: The decay length control sets the length of time it takes for the reverb tail to decay or fade away. Longer decay lengths create a more spacious and ambient sound, while shorter decay lengths create a more tight and focused sound.

3. Pre-delay: The pre-delay control sets the amount of time between the direct sound and the start of the reverb. This can be used to create a sense of distance between the sound source and the reverb, or to create a more defined sense of space.

4. Early reflections: The early reflections control sets the level of the initial reflections that occur immediately after the direct sound. This can be used to create a sense of closeness or distance between the sound source and the reverb.

5. Wetness: The wetness control sets the balance between the dry, unprocessed sound and the wet, reverberant sound. Lower wetness values result in less reverb and a dryer sound, while higher wetness values result in more reverb and a wetter sound.

To use reverb in synthwave music, you might want to start with a shorter decay time, to create a more tight and focused reverb

6.5 How to use a compressor

An audio compressor is a device or software that is used to control the dynamic range of an audio signal by reducing the level of loud sounds and increasing the level of quiet sounds. This can be useful for a variety of applications, such as mixing, mastering, and live sound reinforcement.

A typical audio compressor has several controls that can be adjusted to achieve the desired amount of compression:

1. Threshold: The threshold control sets the level at which the compressor begins to reduce the level of the audio signal. Any signal that exceeds the threshold level will be affected by the compression.

2. Ratio: The ratio control sets the amount of compression applied to the audio signal. A ratio of 2:1 means that for every 2 dB above the threshold level, the output level will be increased by 1 dB. Higher ratios result in more compression, while lower ratios result in less compression.

3. Attack: The attack control sets the amount of time it takes for the compressor to begin reducing the level of the audio signal once it exceeds the threshold. A shorter attack time results in more immediate compression, while a longer attack time results in more gradual compression.

4. Release: The release control sets the amount of time it takes for the compressor to stop reducing the level of the audio signal once it falls back below the threshold. A shorter release time results in more immediate release, while a longer release time results in more gradual release.

5. Knee: The knee control determines the transition from uncompressed to compressed audio. A hard knee will quickly transition from uncompressed to compressed audio, while a soft knee will gradually transition, resulting in a more subtle compression effect.

6. Make-up gain: This control allows you to adjust the overall output level of the audio signal after compression. This is useful to compensate for any perceived loss of level caused by the compression.

To use an audio compressor, you would start by setting the threshold control to a level that is appropriate for the audio signal you are working with. Then, adjust the ratio control to achieve the desired amount of compression. Next, adjust the attack and release controls to fine-tune the timing of the compression. Finally, adjust the make-up gain to bring the overall level of the audio signal back to where it was before compression.

It's important to remember that compression is a tool that should be used sparingly and with care, as overcompression can result in a loss of dynamic range and a "squashed" sound. It's always good to listen to the audio before and after applying the compression and make adjustments accordingly.

6.6 Compression and Limiting while Mixing

Compression and limiting are important tools when mixing synthwave music. They are used to control the dynamic range of a track and to add punch and power to the mix. Here are some tips for using compression and limiting when mixing synthwave music:

1. Use compression to control the dynamic range: Compression is used to control the dynamic range of a track by reducing the difference in volume between the loudest and softest parts of a track. This helps to make the track sound more consistent and polished.

2. Use different types of compression: There are different types of compression, such as peak compression and RMS compression. Peak compression is used to control the loudest parts of a track, while RMS compression is used to control the overall level of a track. Experiment with different types of compression to find the right balance for your track.

3. Use compression to add punch and power: Compression can be used to add punch and power to a track by increasing the level of the attack of the track. This makes the track sound more powerful and assertive.

4. Use limiting to prevent clipping: Limiting is used to prevent clipping, which is when the level of a track exceeds the maximum level that can be recorded or played back. Clipping can cause distortion and make the track sound unpleasant.

5. Use parallel compression: Parallel compression is the process of routing a sound through multiple compressors at the same time. This can be used to add punch and power to a track while still preserving the dynamic range.

6. Experiment with different settings: Experiment with different compression and limiting settings to find the right balance for your track. Try adjusting the threshold, ratio, attack, release, and makeup gain to find the right balance for your track.

7. Use software compression: Software compression is a powerful tool for mixing and mastering. There are a variety of software compressors available, such as the UAD 1176, and the Waves SSL 4000. These software compressors can provide a wide range of compression settings that can be used to shape the sound of your track.

Compression and limiting are important tools when mixing synthwave music. They are used to control the dynamic range of a track and to add punch and power to the mix. Experimenting with different types of compression, parallel compression, different settings, and software compression can help you to create a cohesive and polished sound that is typical of synthwave music.

6.7 My basic theory of mastering

Mastering isn't too hard either, once you get the hang of it. A lot of people try to sell it like it's some super-esoteric thing, but it really isn't. It is, however, not to be taken lightly as it is a complete job unto itself. Mastering is the easiest and quickest way to ruin a perfectly good sounding track. It's also something that must be done, as your track won't really sound "finished" until it is mastered.

My basic theory on mastering is actually shockingly cliche; "garbage in, garbage out", followed by "make it loud enough". I realize that the first platitude is a bit tiring, and probably applies to every other step in the song-creation process as well, but I feel along with the qualifier "make it loud enough", it really does capture the heart of what mastering is. If your mix is good, and your monitors are true, you will have a fairly easy time mastering your track. If up until this point you have taken great care to craft a decent song, meaning; you've written good parts, arranged and performed them well, and have filled out the frequency spectrum with an even and balanced "mix"... then you should be 96% there. If your mixing stage has left you with instruments that are balanced, audible, and "sweetened" with just the right amount of effects and EQ tailoring, then your job at the mastering stage is really focused on "making it loud enough".

Oftentimes, here at the mastering stage, engineers get carried away with additional "sweetening", since you can certainly do a lot to the overall mix with modern hi-fidelity mastering plug-ins. You can certainly boost, cut, compress, and even adjust the stereo width of the overall track. These things, to varying degrees, can definitely make thighs sound subjectively "better", but should not be used to correct mistakes that were made in the mixing stage. If so, you're going to end up with an inferior sounding final track (trust me).

With that said, you can also make the argument that mastering *is* the art of making subtle fixes to the mix, for exactly that reason- to adjust things that for whatever reason, need adjusting (no mix is perfect). There are many, many professional mastering engineers (and I'm talking about the top guys in Hollywood) who have some shocking stories of receiving mixes in varying states of subpar sound that they historically had to repair, and went on to become hit songs.

So beyond the basics of "garbage in, garbage out", here's what you might say is my *actual* advice on mastering; Don't screw it up. Sweeten it a bit if you need to, and fix any objective issues with the sound, like missing parts of the frequency spectrum that need to be addressed, or left/right balance issues. Of course, bring the overall level (volume) up by an appropriate amount, but try to do this while preserving the mix's overall dynamic range and clarity. In other words, if you must compress and limit during the mastering stage, please stop and pull back before anything begins to overload or distort.

Really, the adjustments you are making at the mastering stage (if any) are going to be VERY minute. Think about adjustments on the order of 0.5 decibels or so. Maybe 1.5 or 2 dB if you're being sort of extreme. With EQ on the overall track, I tend to add EQ (make slight boosts in gain) rather than making cuts. This is counter to what I do during the mix stage, but it's advice that I've learned from some of the top modern mastering "gurus". The logic behind this is that you don't want to "take away" information from the final mix (which is assumed to be a good final mix). As long as there is ample headroom in the mix (meaning that the volume is not already maxed-out near zero dB), then any deficiencies in the spectrum can be addressed by adding what isn't quite there.

Similarly, adjustments in compression and limiting should be very subtle. Minimal compression ratios of 1:1.1 or 1:1.2 are common in mastering. As are limiting and compression thresholds of -1 or -2 dB. In other words, you want your dynamics to be altered just at their very peaks. If you squish your signal down further, you can hear the compression as an effect, and it doesn't sound pleasant. Often limiters can "pump" causing awful spikes and dropouts. At the end of the day, none of this sounds natural and should be avoided. Remember, that effects during the mastering stage are affecting EVERYTHING in the mix together, and as said in the beginning of this chapter, poor mastering choices are the fastest way to ruin a perfectly good song.

When in doubt (during the mastering stage), turn things down. Set your EQs, limiters and compressors to "off", or start setting the knobs closer to "0". If you hear distortion, follow your gain staging, and find out where your signal is getting loud, and turn it down there. Try to get things to sound "natural", and then slowly raise your gain until it's close to where it needs to be.

Re-visit your compressor and limiter settings, and re-adjust as necessary. Perhaps you don't even need your compressor while mastering. Sweeten the EQ as necessary, use bell-shaped parametric EQs to really hone in on certain regions. Use high and low shelves to add overall high or low frequencies in more extreme cases. At all times, strive for a clean, consistent sound that's "true" to the original mix.

6.8 Understanding LUFS

The LUFS (Loudness Units Full Scale) scale is a measurement unit for audio loudness that considers the perceived loudness of a sound. It's becoming increasingly important in the audio industry as it provides a standardized way to measure the perceived loudness of a track, taking into account various factors such as human hearing sensitivity, psychoacoustics, and listening environment.

LUFS is calculated based on a statistical evaluation of the average loudness of an audio signal and is used to measure loudness over a specific period of time. In other words, it's a measure of how loud an audio track sounds to the average listener, rather than just its maximum volume. In a DAW, you can typically find the LUFS measurement on a decibel meter located on the master bus. To read the LUFS output, you look at the scale on the meter, which is usually marked in units of LUFS, and then find the decibel value that the meter is showing. The higher the decibel value, the louder the audio track.

Most other books and resources on the subject will tell you to master your track to -14 LUFS. I don't recommend this, and here's why; That advice is based on the supposition that online streaming services will "normalize" your track to -14 LUFS, and that anything louder is just going to be "turned down". In reality, that is only partially true. Spotify (arguably the most popular streaming service for synthwave) only normalizes to -14 when played back on a mobile device, or if the listener has their "normalized volume" setting turned on. If not, as in the case of many home-stereo systems, the dynamic range will be much higher. In these cases, songs mastered to -14 LUFS will sound quieter and flat compared to something mastered louder. **The real maximum volume that you are shooting for is -8 LUFS. This is what nearly all of today's record labels and professional clients request for masters being sent out to streaming platforms.**

6.9 Compression and Limiting while Mastering

Compression and limiting are important tools when mastering synthwave music. They are used to control the dynamic range of a track and to add loudness and clarity to the final mix. Here are some tips for using compression and limiting when mastering synthwave music:

1. Use compression to control the dynamic range: Compression is used to control the dynamic range of a track by reducing the difference in volume between the loudest and softest parts of a track. This helps to make the track sound more consistent and polished.

2. Use limiting to increase loudness: Limiting is used to increase the loudness of a track. A limiter is a type of compressor that is set to a high ratio and a low threshold, which allows the loudest parts of a track to be amplified without causing distortion.

3. Use multiband compression: Multiband compression is a technique where different frequency bands are compressed separately. This allows for more precise control of the dynamic range and can help to enhance the perceived loudness of the track.

4. Use stereo imaging: Stereo imaging can be used to enhance the perceived loudness of a track. Try using stereo imaging techniques to create a sense of depth and space in your mix.

5. Use a mastering EQ: Mastering EQ is a specialized EQ that is used to balance the frequencies of a track. This can help to enhance the perceived loudness of a track by boosting the frequencies that are important for loudness and clarity.

6. Use a final limiter: A final limiter is used to increase the overall loudness of a track and to prevent clipping. It's important to use a final limiter with care and not to overdo it, as excessive limiting can cause distortion and make the track sound unpleasant.

7. Use software mastering: Software mastering is a powerful tool for mastering. There are a variety of software mastering plugins available such as Ozone 9, and LANDR, which can provide a wide range of mastering tools that can be used to shape the sound of your track.

6.10 Creating a cohesive and polished final mix

Creating a cohesive and polished final mix is an essential step when producing synthwave music. A well-mixed track will have all of its elements working together to create a polished and balanced sound. Here are some tips for creating a cohesive and polished final mix when producing synthwave music:

1. Use a reference track: Use a reference track to compare your mix to a professionally mixed and mastered track. This will help you to identify areas where your mix needs improvement and to make more accurate adjustments.

2. Balance the levels of the different elements: Make sure that the levels of the different elements in your mix are balanced. This will ensure that the different elements are heard clearly and that there are no elements that are overpowering others.

3. Use EQ to balance the frequencies: Use EQ to balance the frequencies of the different elements in your mix. This will ensure that the different elements are heard clearly and that there are no elements that are overpowering others.

4. Use compression: Compression can be used to control the dynamic range of a track and to add punch and power to the mix. Experiment with different compression settings to find the right balance for your track.

5. Use stereo imaging: Use stereo imaging techniques to create a sense of space and depth in your mix. Experiment with panning and stereo width to find the right balance for your track.

6. Use effects: Effects such as reverb and delay can be used to create a sense of space and atmosphere in your mix. Experiment with different effects to find the right balance for your track.

7. Use mastering techniques: Mastering techniques such as compression and limiting can be used to increase the loudness and clarity of your track. Be careful not to overdo it, as excessive compression and limiting can cause distortion and make the track sound unpleasant.

8. Listen in different environments: Listen to your mix in different environments such as on headphones, speakers, and in different rooms. This will help you to identify any issues with your mix and make adjustments accordingly.

9. Get a second opinion: Get a second opinion from a friend or colleague. It can be helpful to have a fresh perspective on your mix and can help you to identify any issues that you may have missed.

Part VII: Promotion and Distribution

7.1 How to get your music heard

Getting your music heard as a synthwave artist can be challenging, but with the right strategies and tools, it's possible to build a following and gain recognition for your work. Here are some tips for getting your music heard as a synthwave artist:

1. Build an online presence: Building an online presence is essential for getting your music heard. Create a website and social media accounts to promote your music, share updates about upcoming releases, and connect with fans.

2. Use streaming platforms: Streaming platforms like Spotify, Apple Music, and YouTube are great ways to get your music heard by a wider audience. Make sure to optimize your profile, upload your music, and engage with your listeners.

3. Submit your music to curators: Curators on platforms like Soundcloud and YouTube can help to promote your music by featuring it on their channels. Reach out to curators that align with your genre and style and submit your music for consideration.

4. Play live: Playing live is a great way to get your music heard and to connect with fans. Look for local venues, festivals, and events where you can play, and consider booking your own show.

5. Collaborate: Collaborating with other artists is a great way to get your music heard. Look for other synthwave artists to collaborate with, and consider working with producers and remixers to create new versions of your songs.

6. Release your music on a regular basis: Releasing your music on a regular basis will help to keep your fans engaged and interested. Consider releasing a new single or EP every few months to keep your followers interested and to build momentum.

7. Network: Networking is key to getting your music heard. Attend local music events, join online groups and forums, and engage with other artists and industry professionals.

8. Use paid promotion: Paid promotion can help to boost your visibility and reach a wider audience. Consider investing in targeted ads, social media promotion, or playlist promotion to help your music reach more listeners.

Getting your music heard as a synthwave artist can be challenging, but with the right strategies and tools, it's possible to build a following and gain recognition for your work. Building an online presence, using streaming platforms, submitting your music to curators, playing live, collaborating, releasing your music on a regular basis, networking, and using paid promotion are key to getting your music heard.

7.2 Building a fanbase

Building a fanbase is a crucial step for any synthwave artist who is self-promoting. A fanbase can provide support, feedback, and help you reach a wider audience. Here are some tips for building a fanbase as a self-promoting synthwave artist:

1. Create and share high-quality content: Creating and sharing high-quality content is essential for building a fanbase. Share your music, videos, photos, and updates about your upcoming releases on your website and social media platforms.

2. Engage with your audience: Engaging with your audience is a key component of building a fanbase. Respond to comments, answer questions, and participate in conversations on your social media platforms.

3. Use social media to your advantage: Social media platforms like Instagram, Twitter, and TikTok are powerful tools for building a fanbase. Use them to share your content, engage with your audience, and connect with other synthwave artists and fans.

4. Host giveaways and contests: Giveaways and contests are great ways to build your fanbase. Host a contest and ask your fans to share their favorite synthwave tracks or give away a free digital download of your music.

5. Offer exclusive content: Offering exclusive content is a great way to build a fanbase. Share behind-the-scenes footage, demos, or rough mixes of your music to give your fans a unique look into your creative process.

6. Collaborate with other synthwave artists: Collaborating with other synthwave artists can help to build your fanbase. Not only will you learn from each other, but also you'll be able to expand your reach by collaborating with other acts that have a fanbase of their own.

7. Play live shows: Playing live shows is a great way to build a fanbase. Look for local venues, festivals, and events where you can play, and consider booking your own show.

8. Build a mailing list: Building a mailing list is a great way to stay in touch with your fanbase. Use your website or social media platforms to collect email addresses and send out updates about new releases, upcoming shows, and exclusive content.

9. Participate in online communities: Participate in online communities such as forums, groups, and Discord channels where synthwave fans and artists gather. Share your music, engage in conversations, and collaborate with other members to build your fanbase.

Building a fanbase is a crucial step for any synthwave artist who is self-promoting. Creating and sharing high-quality content, engaging with your audience, using social media to your advantage, hosting giveaways and contests, offering exclusive content, collaborating with other synthwave artists, playing live shows, building a mailing list, and participating in online communities are key

7.3 Platforms for uploading and distributing music

For self-releasing musicians, uploading and distributing music on different platforms is an essential step to getting their music heard by a wider audience. Here are some of the most popular platforms for uploading and distributing music, and how to use them effectively:

1. Bandcamp: Bandcamp is a popular platform for self-releasing musicians. It allows artists to upload their music, sell physical merchandise, and collect revenue directly from fans. Artists can set their own prices for their music, and can even offer it for free.

2. SoundCloud: SoundCloud is a platform that allows artists to upload, share, and promote their music. Artists can build a following, connect with other musicians and fans, and even make money through the platform's monetization program.

3. YouTube: YouTube is not only a platform for videos but also a great place to share and promote music. Artists can upload their music videos and audio tracks, create playlists, and reach a wide audience. It's also a great place to share live performances, behind the scenes footage, and other content related to their music.

4. Spotify: Spotify is one of the most popular music streaming platforms in the world. Artists can upload their music to the platform and reach a global audience. Spotify also offers a variety of promotional tools, such as playlist curation and targeted advertising, to help artists reach new listeners.

5. Apple Music: Apple Music is a streaming service and platform for music distribution that allows artists to upload and share their music. It also offers a variety of promotional tools and features, such as playlist curation, to help artists reach new listeners.

6. Amazon Music: Amazon Music is a streaming service and platform for music distribution that allows artists to upload and share their music. It also offers a variety of promotional tools and features, such as playlist curation, to help artists reach new listeners.

7. Tidal: Tidal is a streaming service and platform for music distribution that allows artists to upload and share their music. It also offers a variety of promotional tools and features, such as playlist curation, to help artists reach new listeners.

When using these platforms, it's important to optimize your profile, engage with your fans and followers, and use the promotional tools that are offered by the platform. Additionally, it's important to use consistent branding across all platforms, and to promote your music on different platforms in a coordinated manner. It's also important to keep in mind the terms of service and copyright laws of each platform.

7.4 Distrokid and CD Baby

DistroKid and CD Baby are popular distribution platforms that allow independent musicians to upload, publish, and distribute their music to various online music stores and streaming platforms. Both platforms have their own set of features and tools that can be useful for synthwave musicians to get their music heard by a wider audience.

DistroKid is a digital distribution platform that allows musicians to upload their music to a wide range of streaming services, such as Spotify, Apple Music, and Tidal. It also has a feature called "Unlimited," which allows musicians to upload unlimited amounts of music for a yearly fee. With DistroKid, musicians can also set their own prices for their music, and even offer it for free. One of the main benefits of using DistroKid is that it is easy to use and it has a user-friendly interface. Artists can easily upload their music and distribute it to various platforms with just a few clicks. Additionally, DistroKid has a feature called "Splits" that allows multiple people to share in the revenue from a single release. This can be useful for collaborations or for splits with producers, engineers or other contributors.

CD Baby is a digital distribution platform that allows musicians to upload their music to a wide range of streaming services, such as Spotify, Apple Music, and Tidal. It also has a feature called "Pro" which offers additional services such as worldwide distribution, custom UPC and ISRC codes, and sync licensing. CD Baby also has a feature called "Sync Licensing" that allows musicians to license their music for use in TV, film, and other media.

One of the main benefits of using CD Baby is that it has a wide range of distribution options. This can be useful for musicians who want to distribute their music to specific regions, or who want to make their music available on platforms that are not available on other distribution platforms. Additionally, CD Baby has a feature called "YouTube Monetization" that allows musicians to monetize their music on YouTube.

Both DistroKid and CD Baby are popular distribution platforms that allow independent musicians to upload, publish, and distribute their music to various online music stores and streaming platforms. Both platforms have their own set of features and tools that can be useful for

7.5 Bandcamp

Bandcamp is a popular online platform that allows musicians to distribute and sell their music directly to fans, for free. For whatever reason, Bandcamp has caught on within the synthwave community, and is used by a fairly good amount of synthwave producers to self-distribute their music. Synthwave musicians can use Bandcamp to share their music with a global audience and build a fanbase. Here are step-by-step instructions detailing how to create an account and distribute your music on Bandcamp:

1. Create a Bandcamp account: The first step in distributing your music on Bandcamp is to create an account. You will need to provide basic personal information and choose a username. Once you have created an account, you can set up your artist profile and customize your page with a bio, photos, and links to your social media accounts.

2. Upload your music: Once your account is set up, you can begin uploading your music to Bandcamp. You can upload your tracks as MP3, FLAC, or other audio file formats. You can also include cover art, lyrics, and liner notes with each track.

3. Set your pricing: Bandcamp allows you to set your own prices for your music, which means that you can experiment with different pricing models to find what works best for you. You can choose to offer your music for free, or you can set a fixed price or a "name your price" model.

4. Utilize the Bandcamp community: Bandcamp has a large and active community of music fans, so it's a good idea to take advantage of this by engaging with your fans and other musicians on the platform. You can post updates, share behind-the-scenes photos, and interact with fans through comments and direct messages.

5. Use the Bandcamp analytics: Bandcamp provides detailed analytics that show you how many people are listening to your music, where they're from, and how they're discovering your music. This can be a valuable tool for understanding your fanbase and targeting your marketing efforts.

6. Use Bandcamp's marketing tools: Bandcamp provides a variety of marketing tools that can help you promote your music, such as email campaigns, social media integration, and fan messaging. You can also use these tools to create custom landing pages and track the performance of your campaigns.

7. Create merchandise: Bandcamp also allows you to sell merchandise, such as t-shirts, posters, and CDs. This can be a great way to monetize your music and build a fanbase.

8. Connect with other musicians: Bandcamp is a great place to connect with other musicians and collaborate on projects. You can reach out to other artists and see if they're interested in working together.

Bandcamp is a powerful platform that can help synthwave musicians to distribute and sell their music directly to fans. By taking advantage of the platform's features, such as the community, analytics, and marketing tools, you can build a fanbase and monetize your music. Additionally, creating merchandise, connecting with other musicians and using the analytics can help you to improve your promotion strategy and grow your fanbase.

Part VIII: Conclusion

8.1 Recap of key takeaways

So there you have it. The complete theory and practice on "how to make synthwave" in just over 100 pages. I'm sure there's a lot I missed, to be honest, but I'll save that for the next book. To recap what we've learned, it's basically the following:

1. Set-up your studio. Gather your equipment, get everything comfortable, and make sure your audio interface is connected to your computer. Also make sure your DAW is up and running, and you have all necessary plug-ins and software installed.
2. Experiment around with your synths and sounds. See what you have, identify what you like. Keep a list of presets that you plan to use in the future, which can be saved to your synthesizer's user bank.
3. Once you have some musical ideas brewing, start recording! Even if you don't, start with a basic by-the-numbers drum beat and record that first.
4. Be sure to use the DAW's metronome, and record your parts in time. Always keep "snapping" set to on, so that your parts snap to the grid. Use quantization if needed.
5. Then, using our multitrack DAW, overdub a bass synth part. Be creative and improvise, or go with straight 16th notes if you want.
6. Using your bass line as a guide, add chords over it. You can also reverse these steps and record a chord progression first, then overdub your bassline over that. It's up to you.

Repeat steps 3-4 and create another part to your song (you can copy and paste the drum part if you want, but the other parts should be based on a different chord progression). You can do this in the same DAW session, but at an arbitrary point down the timeline, after the first song section you recorded. The goal is to have at least two distinct but similar parts, but if the mood strikes you more sections are of course better.

You now have (at least) an "A" and "B" section to your song. You may have more than that. If so, the goal is to determine which two or three are *the best of them*, and use those as your song's main sections. Trim the recorded track items in your timeline to create perfect 4 or 6 bar loops. Copy and paste these sections so they repeat between 4-16 times.

When trimming down parts to perfect-length blocks, make sure the very first note of the first beat isn't getting cut off. If anything, quantize or shift just this one note (on the first beat) so that the first note accurately lands on the "1" and loops correctly. Also make sure any extra space is cut off the end so that it loops correctly (in a typical 4/4 song, parts will normally be 1, 2, 4, 8, or 16 bars).

After you have your sections looped and repeated, overdub extra musical parts over these sections. This can be any number or manner of leads, stabs, solos, extra rhythmic or melodic embellishments, swells, rises, crashes, drum rolls, percussion, claps, or literally even "bells and whistles". Make sure these additional parts are in time and in key. Trim the parts down to an even length that makes sense.

You now have two song sections (A and B), along with extra embellishments, leads, and instrumentation for each section. Now you have the fun task of arranging the parts together into a coherent sequence that keeps the listener engaged. The trick is to keep everything flowing in a way that is familiar, exciting, and yet not utterly predictable. Remember to impart a sense of scale through the use of dynamics, density, and layering.

After everything is arranged, it's time to mix and master your track.

When you are happy with your sonic output, decide if you want to publish your music. If so, now is the time to consider Distrokid, CD Baby, or other ways of self-distribution.

8.2 Future directions for synthwave music production

Synthwave music production has seen a steady rise in popularity in recent years, and the future of the genre looks bright. Here are some potential directions that synthwave music production may take in the future:

1. Fusion with other genres: Synthwave music has already begun to incorporate elements of other genres such as hip-hop, house, and rock. As the genre continues to evolve, we may see even more fusion with other genres, resulting in a more diverse and eclectic sound.

2. Increased use of AI and machine learning: As technology continues to advance, we may see an increased use of artificial intelligence (AI) and machine learning in synthwave music production. This could lead to more complex and dynamic soundscapes, as well as more unique and experimental sounds.

3. More focus on live performance: Synthwave music has traditionally been associated with electronic dance music, which is often performed live. However, as the genre continues to evolve, we may see an increased focus on live performance, with more emphasis on live instrumentation and live improvisation.

4. Greater use of virtual reality: Virtual reality technology is becoming more widely accessible, and we may see an increased use of VR in synthwave music production. This could lead to more immersive and interactive live performances and music videos.

5. More emphasis on storytelling and concept albums: Synthwave music has traditionally been associated with a nostalgic and retro aesthetic. As the genre continues to evolve, we may see an increased focus on storytelling and concept albums, which will allow musicians to explore more complex and nuanced themes.

6. Greater use of hardware synthesis: Many synthwave musicians use software synthesizers to create their sounds, but we may see an increased use of hardware synthesis in the future. Hardware synthesizers can have a different sound character and warmth that can add a unique touch to the music.

The future of synthwave music production looks bright, and the genre is likely to continue to evolve and incorporate elements from other genres, technology, and live performance. The use of AI and machine learning, virtual reality, hardware synthesis, storytelling and concept albums may become more popular in the coming years. The key for synthwave musicians is to be creative and always look for new ways to push the boundaries of the genre.

8.3 Synthwave is alive and well

At some point in the lifespan of any musical genre, some smart-alec will inevitably ask "is this dead?". Usually this happens long, long before the actual death of said genre. As an example, Lenny Kravitz released the rock song "Rock And Roll Is Dead" in 1995, and that saying had already been a thing for decades at that point. I'm sure Lenny was being sarcastic with that title, and here we are decades later still rockin' out. While there is an objective "lifetime" for most musical and artistic trends, music is in an interesting place due to the state of modern technology. It's a fact that retro and retro-inspired genres are lasting in popularity much longer because of the long-tail effect, and the ubiquity of world-wide distribution for legacy media.

When people ask "is synthwave dead" in reference to the musical genre, they are referring to the question of whether the popularity and relevance of synthwave music has declined and whether the genre is no longer being actively produced or consumed- but compared to what?

Some people might argue that synthwave has reached its peak and that the genre has become oversaturated with copycat music and the lack of new, innovative sounds and ideas. They might also argue that the current cultural climate has moved on from the nostalgia-fueled aesthetic of synthwave, and that the genre is no longer as relevant or popular as it once was.

On the other hand, others might argue that synthwave is still alive and well, and that the genre is continuously evolving and growing with new artists and sounds. They might point to the fact that there is still a large and dedicated fanbase for synthwave, and that there is still plenty of new music being produced within the genre.

In general, the question of whether synthwave is "dead" is a highly subjective one, and opinions will vary greatly depending on who you ask. It's important to note that the genre is continuously evolving and changing. New subgenres are emerging, and in my opinion the genre of Synthwave is not dead, but is still very much alive.

8.4 Encouragement to continue experimenting and developing your skills.

As a synthwave musician, it's essential to continue experimenting and developing your skills to keep pushing the boundaries of the genre and stand out in the crowded music scene. Here are some reasons why experimenting and developing your skills is important, and some tips on how to do it:

1. Exploration leads to innovation: Experimenting and trying new things can lead to breakthroughs and new ideas that can help to define and differentiate your sound. By exploring different sounds, techniques, and styles, you'll be able to develop a more unique and innovative sound that sets you apart from others.

2. Keeps the music fresh: Experimentation and development help to keep the music fresh and exciting. It's easy to get stuck in a creative rut and to repeat the same sounds and techniques over and over again. By constantly experimenting and developing new skills, you'll be able to create new and exciting music that keeps your fans engaged.

3. Helps you to stay relevant: The music industry is constantly changing, and new sounds and styles are always emerging. By experimenting and developing your skills, you'll be able to stay relevant and adapt to new trends and changes in the industry.

4. Improves your technical abilities: Experimentation and development can help to improve your technical abilities. By trying new techniques and experimenting with different sounds, you'll be able to develop a better understanding of music production and sound design.

5. Increases your versatility: Experimenting and developing your skills can also increase your versatility as a musician. By exploring different sounds and styles, you'll be able to play different types of gigs and collaborate with other musicians in different genres.

8.5 Tips for creating a sense of nostalgia in your music

Creating a feeling of 1980s nostalgia in synthwave music involves a combination of different elements, including sound design, composition, and production techniques. Here is a detailed yet easy-to-understand essay on how a musician would build a feeling of 1980s nostalgia in their synthwave music:

1. Sound design: One of the key elements in creating a feeling of 1980s nostalgia in synthwave music is the use of retro-inspired sound design. This can include using vintage synthesizers, such as the Roland Jupiter 8 or the Moog Minimoog, or emulating the sounds of these instruments using software synthesizers and plugins. Additionally, it can incorporate sounds from other 1980s technology such as drum machines like Roland TR-808 or TR-909 or Casio VL-1.

2. Composition and harmony: Another important element in creating a feeling of 1980s nostalgia in synthwave music is the use of composition and harmony techniques that were common in the 1980s. This can include using chord progressions and melodies inspired by popular 1980s music, as well as using traditional synthwave chord structures and arpeggios.

3. Production techniques: To further enhance the feeling of 1980s nostalgia in synthwave music, a musician can use production techniques that were common in the 1980s. This can include using vintage effects such as reverb, delay, and flanger, as well as using mixing and mastering techniques that emulate the sound of 1980s recordings.

4. Lyrics and themes: Lastly, a musician can also use lyrics and themes that are reminiscent of the 1980s. This can include references to popular culture, technology, and events that were prevalent during the decade.

Creating a feeling of 1980s nostalgia in synthwave music involves a combination of different elements, including sound design, composition, and production techniques, that are inspired by the music and culture of the 1980s. By incorporating these elements, a musician can effectively evoke a sense of nostalgia and transport listeners back to the era.

8.6 Tips on how to experiment and develop your skills as a synthwave musician:

1. Learn new instruments: In my opinion, the goal for synthwave styled music would be playing keyboards (synthesizers), guitar, and also being able to sing- that's the synthwave production "triple threat". Even if you're already at that level, learning a new instrument can open up new possibilities for your music. Even if you don't plan on using the instrument in your music, learning it can help to improve your understanding of music and inspire new ideas. If you play guitar at all, it can be very beneficial to pick up a bass guitar, and vice-versa. If you're a keyboard super-enthusiast, there's a world of controller options out there; everything from MPC pad and grid style MIDI controllers, to MPE equipped keyboards (such as the ROLI Rise and Lumi). I realize that a lot of

synthesizer players are set in their preferences, but stepping out of your comfort zone for the sake of inspiration is kind of the point here. Try it!

2. Take Lessons: Whether it's learning a new instrument or learning audio engineering, you can certainly teach yourself. However, your progress will probably go lightyears farther if you take private lessons from a high-level teacher.

3. Try different software and recording techniques: While I tried to pack as much knowledge as I could into this book, there's always much more to learn. There are so many options for software and plug-ins, and so many ways to approach the same thing. This applies both to the recording and to the music composition itself. Different approaches have their own strengths and weaknesses. Effects and virtual instruments almost always have a signature sound, and it can be inspiring to try a new sonic palette. This can mean trying free plug-ins, or splurging on hardware/software just to try something new. Similarly, techniques in tracking and mixing are also nearly infinite, and sometimes taking an alternate path can lead to interesting and happy accidents.

4. Stay tuned to new info: In order to stay inspired and learn new things, subscribing to "record production" social media can go a long way. Rather than focusing on the random and usually bad advice found in groups and forums, I would recommend finding and following an actual producer on social media that you trust, and who regularly uploads quality "how to" content. While most of the producers in this category are probably going to be "influencer producers" rather than working guys making platinum records, there are still more than enough folks out there who know what they're doing, and are absolutely creating good content that you can learn from.. There are a lot of these types of channels on YouTube, and they cover literally every genre and style of music.

Made in the USA
Monee, IL
15 August 2025

23407547R00059